D0900077

ONE AND HOLY

ONE AND HOLY

by

KARL ADAM

Translated by
CECILY HASTINGS

SHEED AND WARD
LONDON AND NEW YORK

FIRST PUBLISHED 1954
BY SHEED AND WARD, LTD.
33 MAIDEN LANE
LONDON, W.C.2
AND
SHEED AND WARD, INC.
840 BROADWAY,
NEW YORK, 3

NIHIL OBSTAT: MICHAEL P. NOONAN, S.M.
CENSOR DEPUTATUS

IMPRIMATUR: ✠ RICHARD J. CUSHING
ARCHBISHOP OF BOSTON

BOSTON, MARCH 22, 1951

PRINTED IN GREAT BRITAIN
BY PURNELL AND SONS, LTD.
PAULTON (SOMERSET) AND LONDON

FOREWORD

THE FOLLOWING lectures were first delivered to a large gathering of the *Una Sancta* movement at Stuttgart and Karlsruhe. The ideas here advanced are often closely related to those expressed by Johannes Hessen in his stimulating work, *Luther in Katholischer Sicht*. I did not actually see his book until after I had given my lectures. Hessen gives a philosophical and historical account of the "phenomenon of Luther" and the possibility of an ultimate understanding with the Lutheran Church. It is my aim to provide this with a clear theological basis.

It cannot be doubted that at the present moment, under the shattering impact of two world wars, a bridge is being built between Catholics and Lutherans, at least in the sense that the unreality of mere polemic is being abandoned, that Luther on the one hand and the Papacy on the other are being seen in a clearer and more friendly light, and that real efforts are being made, by Christians everywhere, to bring about if not a *unio fidei* at least a *unio caritatis*.

Since Luther can only be understood against the background of the ecclesiastical abuses of the late Middle Ages, I could not avoid dealing with these abuses in detail. I have deliberately taken my evidence exclusively from Catholic sources, especially from Karl Bihlmeyer's history of the Church (the objectivity and thoroughness of which have made it the standard work on the subject), and Josef Lortz's brilliant and psychologically penetrating *Reformation in Deutschland*. In the light of recent researches it should hardly be necessary to emphasise that these abuses do not give the whole picture of the mediaeval Church. Its darker aspects are relieved by so many bright lights that it is not possible to take a pessimistic view of it as a whole.

KARL ADAM

CONTENTS

CONTENTS

I

THE ROOTS OF THE REFORMATION

WE CHRISTIANS have always found it an occasion of suffering that Christendom is divided into a Catholic and a non-Catholic part, a *corpus Catholicorum* and a *corpus Acatholicorum*. Wherever belief in the Son of God made man has remained alive, the Christian conscience has been pierced by the overwhelming reproach and accusation of the High Priest's prayer to the Father on the eve of His Passion: *Ut omnes unum sint*—"that they all may be one, as Thou, Father, in Me and I in Thee!" (John xvii. 21). He reproaches us for so cruel a wounding of His holy Body the Church and for letting centuries go by with these festering divisions among Christians unhealed. He laid on His disciples His new commandment that they should love one another. He formed them into a united company by His own utterly self-giving love for men. And men who love Him must answer today, as for centuries past, for the sin of scandalising the non-Christian world with a shameful example of faction and conflict. "See how they love one another!" said the pagans of the first Christian centuries, when they beheld the loving unity of the early Christians. "See how little they love one another!" the modern pagans might and must say mockingly, as they become more and more conscious of the many deep divisions among Christians.

Even when the Reformation was a thing long established there were men who strove continually to realise that last and deepest desire of their Lord: *ut omnes unum sint.* We need only remember the efforts towards unity of Hugo Grotius (d. 1645) and Leibnitz (d. 1716) on the one side, of Bossuet, Bishop of Meaux (d. 1704) and the Franciscan Spinola, Bishop of Wiener-Neustadt (d. 1695) on the other. These attempts all came to nothing. They were always thwarted by the fact that there were men on both sides who were not inspired simply by the one Spirit of the Lord, the πνεῦμα ἅγιον, but by alien spirits, the πνεύματα of men, with their different aims and exigencies and desires, arising out of their various nationalities and cultures, their differences in temperament and in religious approach.

Must it always be so? Unity was our Lord's legacy to His disciples, attested in prayer before the face of the triune God and hallowed by the sacrificial death which He accepted for their sake. Is it further to remain for so many who love Him an empty wish and a dead word, a reproach not only to us but to Christianity? Now, if ever, is the time to shake ourselves out of our spiritual torpor and religious indifference, and to plunge our consciences into the very heart of Jesus, into the ultimate depths of the intentions bequeathed to us by the God-Man. We Christians have just passed through a time when religious disunity drove us to the very brink of the abyss. A set of godless men, hating Christ as the Son of David, almost succeeded in rooting out from the German people not merely this or that Christian denomination but the very *substance* of Christianity itself. And this was because our people were unable to gather with closed ranks round the

Cross of our Lord and to confess with one heart and one mouth their *Credo* in Jesus Christ.

After these bitter experiences, a *rapprochement* between the Christian denominations—and ultimately a full, external reunion—can no longer be regarded, so far as Germans are concerned, as the desire of a few idealistic and far-seeing souls alone. For German Christianity it has become a vital question, a choice of "to be or not to be" for the *Christian substance* in our people, and so in the heart of Europe. We know that organised anti-Christianity lies in wait beyond our frontiers. We must recognise that there is in our midst something even more dangerous, carrying a far greater menace of ruin—the vacuum that has been left in the German soul: an emptiness, a fearful emancipation from all memories, traditions and ideals of Christianity, making room for every demon of heart and mind and preparing the soul to receive any and every gospel, not only the Gospel of the Cross. How can German Christianity hold its ground against this anti-Christianity without and within, how can it arm itself against the gates of Hell, when it is split to its very core? When, conscious of this disunity, it cannot even pray with a clear conscience to our Lord Jesus Christ? When it can no longer summon up the power to bear witness in one united confession to our Lord and Saviour?

To-day, then, the need, the longing and the clamour for unity have become the heritage of the Christian masses, as simple and elementary as any basic need. On all sides groups are forming whose one longing is for reunion. No longer is it thought that the fulfilment and realisation of our Lord's longing that there should be one fold might be left solely to ecclesiastical leaders and their immediate subordinates. Pope and bishop, prelate and superior have certainly the heaviest responsibility for seeing that Christ shall not have prayed in vain. But this responsibility rests upon us too, upon *us*, Christian workers and peasants, officials and clergy, upon *us*, men and women, old and young. One single vast wave of longing for unity, of will to unity, must arise in German Christianity, must carry up and sweep along with it all our faith and all our devotion, and at last grow to a movement of such depth and breadth that even cold and indifferent Christians will be swept into it. Once this has happened, our will to unity will itself produce a way of accomplishing it.

It is my task in the following lectures to throw some light on this way.

Let me say at once that the way, seen as a whole, is wearisome and hard. A mere longing for unity is not enough. Each of us, in our different circumstances, must help to prepare for it. And it is surely true that we shall best show our loyalty to Jesus by refusing to let hindrances and difficulties keep us from seeking and following the road to unity. For there are hindrances and difficulties. Reunion is not a matter of simple goodwill only, but also of hard thinking and energetic action. More precisely, we need a kind of goodwill which is ready to abandon deep-seated prejudices and habits of thought for the sake of eternal truth, and is willing to go unconditionally to the very ground of truth itself.

The way is a way of blood and wounds, both for the Catholic and for the Protestant, though differently for each of them. It is only by surveying its approaches and its difficulties in the light of history that we can understand why we cannot as yet hope that all Christendom may be finally gathered into one in the near future and also why it was that our Lord prayed specially for unity and bequeathed it as a legacy to His disciples. It was made a special prayer and legacy of our Lord because it is, in the last analysis, God's affair. But it is nevertheless for us to prepare the way for a return within that unity of all who truly love Christ.

We will divide the whole complex of problems which here arise into three basic questions: How did German Christianity come to be divided? Is a reunion possible in principle? How can it be achieved?

How did German Christianity come to be divided?

Modern historians are agreed that the roots of the Reformation reach far back into the high Middle Ages. The former monk of Cluny, Gregory VII, in his zeal for the liberty and reform of the Church, so interpreted the papal claims formulated by Augustine, Gregory the Great and Nicholas I that right up into the late Middle Ages they excited repeated resistance from the secular powers, shook the prestige of the Papal See and so prepared the way for Luther's Reformation. Gregory's *Dictatus Papae*, in which he claimed for the Pope a direct authority even over secular affairs, with the right to depose unworthy princes and release their subjects from their oath of allegiance, inspired papal policy all through the Middle Ages.

This certainly added a corrosive bitterness and a devastating violence—a violence which did not stop short of the Papal See itself—to the conflicts which in any event would have been bitter enough between *Regnum* and *Sacerdotium*, the struggle between the Emperor Henry IV and the Pope over investitures, the battles with the Hohenstaufen, Frederick Barbarossa and Frederick II, the conflicts with Philip the Fair of France and Ludwig of Bavaria. In Frederick II's Manifesto of 1230 Gregory IX is already branded as "the great Dragon and Antichrist of the last days". In 1301 Philip the Fair had Boniface VIII's Bull *Ausculta* publicly burned, and in 1303 had the Pope himself taken into custody as a "heretic, blasphemer and simoniac." Ludwig of Bavaria, supported by the Franciscan Spirituals, declared Pope John XXII a "formal heretic" in the Reichstag at Nuremberg in 1323.

The counter-attack of the "spiritual sword" was a series of excommunications, extending to the fourth degree of kindred, and years of interdict over whole countries. Germany alone was under interdict for twenty years, which meant that no public religious service could be held, no sacrament could be publicly administered, no bell could sound. The more often these ecclesiastical penalties were imposed, the blunter grew the spiritual sword. Inevitably the religion and morality of the people suffered serious damage, their sense of the Church was weakened, their sympathies were alienated from Christ's vicar. In due course there arose theologians amongst the Franciscan Spirituals, particularly their General Michael of Cesena, and William of Ockham, who in numerous writings questioned the founding by Christ of the Papacy as the Church knows it. And Marsilius of Padua in 1324 drew up a revolutionary programme entitled *Defensor Pacis* with a theory of Church and State which broke completely with traditional mediaeval thought and existing ecclesiastical constitutions—"a significant prelude to the Reformation" (Bihlmeyer II, 356).

Anti-papal feeling in Germany gained ground when the See of Rome moved to Avignon and was thus brought completely under French influence, and again when the financial burdens arising out of the double establishment at Rome and Avignon compelled the Pope to build up a system of taxation which, when expanded, weighed heavily both on spiritual and on economic life. The Camera Apostolica covered the whole Church with a net of taxation called the Census.

Besides the revenues of the Papal State, this included pallium-money (the tax paid by newly appointed Archbishops, Bishops and Abbots), *spolia* (the total assets of deceased prelates), the numerous administrative taxes and procurations for papal visitations; above all, the taxes on the revenues of vacant benefices and annates (payment of the first year's income, or at least half of it, from all ecclesiastical appointments made by the Pope). Since Clement IV had claimed for the Pope unlimited authority over all ecclesiastical appointments in Christendom, the number of benefices reserved to the Pope had risen beyond computation. This aroused general opposition, especially when John XXII, in the course of his conflict with Ludwig of Bavaria, tried to fill all the vacant sees and offices in Germany with his own supporters.

In a similar spirit, but contrary to prevailing ecclesiastical law, the Papal Chancellory in the fourteenth and fifteenth centuries encouraged *cumulus beneficiorum*, i.e., the holding of many benefices by one person, and commendation, by which a benefice could be conferred simply for the income derived from it, without the holder's having any spiritual obligations to fulfil. Moreover the Pope could promise to provide a person to a benefice even before its present occupant had actually died. The spirit of mammon had won such an ascendancy in the Curia that Pope Clement VII, for example, at the very height of the Reformation storm, was trying to make money from the sale of Cardinals' hats. It is against this background that we must understand the denunciation of the great preacher Geiler von Kaisersberg: "It is no longer the Holy Ghost Who appoints the rulers of the Church, but the Devil, and for money, for favour and by bribery of the Cardinals."[1]

---

[1] A less severe judgment on this matter is given by Barraclough, *Papal Provisions*. (Trans.)

It is easily understandable that the Curia's irresponsible policies in matters of taxation and appointments, together with the arbitrary occupation of ecclesiastical offices in Germany by foreigners, gravely limited orderly diocesan government, and that they aroused on all sides uncertainty in regard to the law and consequent discontent amounting to unrest and resistance. There were expensive lawsuits that had to be taken to the highest papal court, the Roman Rota. The German nation had its public grievances (*gravamina nationis Germanicae*). They were raised for the first time in 1456 by Archbishop Dietrich of Mainz at the Fürstentag at Frankfurt. From then on they came up again and again in the Reichstag in the form in which the humanist Jakob Wimpfeling had consolidated them. But the abuses, so far from being removed, mounted from year to year as the papal requirements increased. The Pope's yearly income was greater than that of any German Emperor. John XXII, for instance, died leaving three-quarters of a million gold coins in his treasury: a figure so high, considering the values and conditions of the time, that it was bound to have a catastrophic effect on the believer when he pictured against this background the poor tent-maker Paul or the still poorer fisherman Peter coming with dusty sandals to Rome and bringing nothing with them but a deep and noble desire to preach Christ and to die for Christ.

If the fiscal policy of Avignon, where the Popes had their court for sixty-five years, seriously damaged the political and economic interests of German Christianity and so at least indirectly undermined the religious authority of the Pope, the great Schism of the West, from 1378 to 1417, threatened the prestige of the Papacy with final extinction.

In opposition to Urban VI, elected under pressure from the Roman people and disliked for various reasons, the French

Cardinals in Avignon, the so-called "ultramontani", declaring the election unfree and invalid, raised a cousin of the French King to the papal chair as Clement VII, and Christendom was split into two camps. The division went right through the Christian Body. Whole orders, such as the Cistercians, Carthusians, Franciscans, Dominicans and Carmelites, fell into two halves. And since both Popes excommunicated each other and each other's supporters, the whole of Christendom was at least nominally excommunicate. The split did not come to an end with the deaths of the two Popes, for the Cardinals in Rome and Avignon each obstinately held their own papal elections. Matters grew worse when the Council of Pisa, in 1409, deposed both the Rome and the Avignon Popes as "notorious schismatics and heretics" and elected a third, Alexander V, who soon died, and was followed by John XXIII. Since both the deposed Popes obstinately maintained the validity of their elections this led, not to unity, but "from wicked duality to accursed triplicity". It was only in 1417, with the election of Martin V at the Council of Constance, that the Church could acknowledge one single head again in place of the three previously elected claimants.

It was inevitable that this schism of nearly forty years should shake the Church to her foundation; that radicals of the type of William of Ockham and Marsilius of Padua should formulate a democratic theory of the Church, taking the plenitude of ecclesiastical authority to rest in the body of the faithful, not in a single head; that thoughtful theologians such as Peter d'Ailly and the distinguished John Gerson should construct the so-called conciliar theory, making the Pope subordinate to a General Council and giving the Church a parliamentary instead of a monarchical constitution. The idea of the Church received from the Fathers—in which there was but *one* Rock,

B

one Keeper of the Keys, *one* Shepherd—began to weaken. Trust in the Father of Christendom was gone. In this sense, the experience of the Great Schism had impressed its decisive stamp on the minds of the faithful (Lortz).

Hard upon the dogmatic attack on papal authority inevitably conjured up by the Great Western Schism, there followed its moral collapse; the Renaissance Popes seem to have carried out in their own lives that cult of idolatrous humanism, demonic ambition and unrestrained sensuality which was in many ways bound up with the reawakening of the ancient ideal of manhood. The most sober ecclesiastical historians agree that the reigns of the Popes from Sixtus IV to Leo X "represent, from the religious and ecclesiastical point of view, the lowest level of the Papacy since the tenth and eleventh centuries" (Bihlmeyer II, 477). The unbridled nepotism of Sixtus IV, which threatened to degrade the Papacy to "a dynastic heritage and the *Patrimonium Petri* to a petty Italian state" (Lortz I, 75), was followed by the fateful Bull against Witches issued by Innocent VIII, a man of scandalous life. Worse still was the conduct of Alexander VI, stained with murder and impurity, and the demonic lust for blood and power of his son Cesare Borgia. Then came the burning of the Dominican Savonarola at Alexander's orders, the sheer political jugglery of Julius II, whose pontificate was dissipated in campaigns and wars, and finally the pleasure-loving world-liness of Leo X, who found the chase and the theatre more important than Martin Luther and his religious aspirations. The reputation of the Papacy was dragged not merely in the dust but in the mud. It is especially significant of the mentality of Leo X and of the Renaissance Popes in general, that in the solemn procession at his enthronement in the papal chair, the Most Blessed Sacrament was accompanied by statues of naked pagan gods, with the inscription "First Venus reigned [the age of Alexander VI], then Mars [in the time of Julius II], and now [under Leo X] Pallas Athene holds the sceptre" (Lortz I, 86).

The news of these scandalous doings, of course, soon crossed the Alps and stripped the last vestige of credit from the Mother of Christendom. The humanist circles at Erfurt and Florence took care of that, and so later did Ulrich von Hutten and the Dunkelmänner letters. Nor was Luther himself far behind them. Even when he was translating the Bible in 1522, before he had reached the hey-day of his hatred for Rome, he depicted the great Harlot of the Apocalypse as wearing the triple papal crown.

Let us turn now from the crying scandals surrounding the highest ecclesiastical authority to the abuses which marred the German Church and her spiritual life before Luther's advent. It is certainly not true to say that the German Church which witnessed these scandals in the Roman government was herself ripe for destruction. The constant urge for reform and the tremendous response when Luther raised the alarm would be incomprehensible if Christian life had died out completely. We can even assert that German Christianity in the last phase of the Middle Ages was, in spite of all, more devout than it is to-day. For to-day a denunciation of abuses by a Martin Luther would cause no revolution. It was the age of the three Catherines, of Siena, Bologna and Genoa; the age when Saint Bridget scourged the abuses of the Avignon Curia with the flames of her wrath, when Thomas à Kempis wrote his immortal *Imitation of Christ*, when an unknown priest wrote the *Theologia Germanica* first published by Luther. It was the age in which German mysticism flowered in Eckhardt,

Tauler and Suso, and the *devotio moderna* of the "Brothers of the Common Life" was aspiring to revivify, spiritualise and personalise benumbed Christianity. The evidence grows greater and greater that even the common people of the Church, so long as they had not fallen a prey to sectarianism or been touched by radical humanism, were genuinely devoted to their Catholic faith despite all the abuses, and that daily life remained embedded in religious usage right up to the end of the Middle Ages. Even the simple people then knew how to distinguish between the office and the person's own piety and to apply our Lord's words to the gloomy contemporary scene: "All things therefore whatsoever they shall say to you, observe and do; but according to their works do ye not" (Matt. xxiii. 3). During this same second half of the fifteenth century, there was an abundance of pious works *ad remedium animae* (for the welfare of souls): new churches were built, new parishes opened, new appointments of preachers made and charitable institutions set up. New religious and charitable brotherhoods were formed, and even new devotions intro-duced, such as the *Angelus* and the Way of the Cross. There was more catechetical and devotional literature than ever. Booklets and examinations of conscience for Confession, catechism tables, Bible story-books, rhymed Bibles, poor men's Bibles, appeared in the service of religious instruction. Before 1518 a translation of the Bible into High German had run into fourteen editions and one in Low German into four editions. All in all one can fairly speak of an increase of piety in this period. Yet it was seriously lacking in the inner spirit, in the living penetration of pious practices with the spirit of the Gospel. There was too much externalism, too much mere automatism and superficiality, and also far too much unhealthy emotionalism in this piety.

The shepherds and teachers who might have directed and deepened the stream of faith were lacking. The higher clergy were mostly noblemen who had entered the priesthood from material rather than spiritual motives. Bishoprics, prelacies and abbacies had for long been the preserve of the nobility. At the outbreak of the Reformation eighteen bishoprics and archbishoprics in Germany were occupied by the sons of princes. Proof of proficiency in the tourney was an absolutely requisite qualification for most canonries. It is evident that prelates so immersed in worldliness and pleasure had neither the ability nor the desire to break the Bread of Life to the people.

Over against these prelates, "God's Junkers", we see the lower clergy. They seldom had benefices of their own and were compelled either to carry out the duties of a benefice for a pittance from some member of the higher clergy, or earn their living by helping to serve Mass and doing odd jobs about the church. Their economic position was therefore extremely precarious. Their theological training was no better. Excepting the handful of the clergy who were educated at the universities, most of them contented themselves with a modest smattering of religion, Latin and liturgy. Their morals were not much better than their theological knowledge. One could hardly expect a higher moral standard from them than the example set by their superiors. Documentary evidence indicates that there was amongst them much brutality, drunkenness, gambling, avarice, simony and superstition. To secure a living for themselves they exacted almost insupportable fees for the slightest exercise of their priesthood, even from the poor and destitute. The charge for the administration of the Last Sacraments was so high that Extreme Unction was called "the Sacrament of the rich". Concubinage was so general that at the Councils of Constance and Basel the Emperor Sigismund proposed the abolition of the law of celibacy. Amidst the general decline there were still of course plenty of morally upright priests. The humanist Jakob Wimpfeling, a severely critical observer of the life of the Church, vouched "before God" to knowing in the six dioceses of the Rhine "many, nay innumerable, chaste and learned prelates and clergy, of unblemished reputation, full of piety, liberality and care for the poor" (Lortz I, 90). We need only call to mind the illustrious figure of the saintly Nicholas of Cusa, the herald of the modern age and tireless reformer, who sought over and over again by visitations, by word of mouth, and in his writings, to communicate his own spirit of piety to the German Church. But to most of the clergy we must apply the words of Pope Adrian VI in his first consistorial address, quoting from St. Bernard: "Vice has grown so much a matter of course that those who are stained with it are no longer aware of the stink of sin."

The regular clergy were no better than the seculars. Here too we must, of course, beware of false generalisations. It was precisely in this second half of the fifteenth century that almost all the older Orders made an effort to reform. In the case of the Benedictines there were, for example, the reforms of Kastl, Melk and Bursfeld. All the Mendicant Orders still had houses in which the original lofty spirit of the love of God and neighbour was alive. And again and again a saint would arise somewhere in the Church, like Bernardine of Siena, Capistran the lover of souls, and the noble Caritas Pirkheimer, who were shining examples of Christian piety. Luther's account of his own experiences in the Augustinian Priory at Erfurt gives the lie to the statement that monastic discipline was in a universal decline. It is also significant that later on it was ex-monks in particular who were among Luther's best co-operators—who were among the most impatient, in fact, of current abuses. Nevertheless we have from within the Church enough official and unofficial testimony to give us a gloomy picture of life in the Orders. Amongst the more ancient Orders only the Carthusians and in part the Cistercians really maintained their original standard. In the other monasteries there was a tragic decline in discipline. The great Benedictine Abbeys had become a mere convenience of the nobility. But in the Mendicant Orders, too, the foundations of the religious life had begun to totter—not least on account of the irresponsible caprice with which the officials of the Curia at Avignon dispensed religious from the existing rules of the Order or abolished them altogether. Monks and nuns outside the cloister were already a familiar sight in the fifteenth century, and in the sixteenth the begging Friars obtained general permission from Rome to live outside their priories. Community life, and especially community prayer, fell into disuse. So did voluntary poverty. Many of the monks retained their inherited estates and bought or inherited their own cells in the monastery. Erasmus of Rotterdam in his *Enchiridion* singles out for blame their lovelessness and their avarice. Other moral transgressions must be added. The Béguines, for instance, had won for themselves the nickname of "the Friars' cellaresses". The sister of Duke Magnus was known among the rich Clares of Ribnitz as *impudicissima abbatissa*.

It is not to be wondered at that the "Shaven-heads", as the monks were called, were despised and hated by the people, all the more because they were patently increasing in numbers. Together with the lower clergy and the wandering scholars, the "stormy petrels of the revolution", they formed a clerical proletariat. Johannes Agricola estimated the total number of clergy and religious in Germany at the time—in a small total population—at one million four hundred thousand (Lortz I, 86). It cannot be doubted that the majority of this clerical proletariat had neither the intellectual nor the moral capacity to so much as guess the profundity of the questions raised by Luther, let alone fully to realise the gravity of the challenge and to counter it with an adequate response.

Omne malum a clero—every evil comes from the clergy. As early as 1245 at the Council of Lyons Pope Innocent IV had called the sins of the higher and lower clergy one of the five wounds in the Body of the Church, and at the second Council of Lyons in 1274 Gregory X declared that the wickedness of many prelates was the cause of the ruin of the whole world (cf. Bihlmeyer II, 336). Machiavelli, again, speaks volumes in the sarcastic remark that "We Italians may thank the Church and our priests that we have become irreligious and wicked" (Lortz I, 119).

In this waste of clerical corruption it was impossible for the spirit of our Lord to penetrate into the people, take root there and bring true religion to flower. Since there was at this time no catechism of infants, the sermons on Sundays and feast-days were the chief sources from which the laity drew their religious education. And these sources were often choked up. Since at this time, moreover, as during the whole of the Middle Ages, Communion was very infrequent outside the ranks of the mystics, there was no sacramental impulse towards an interiorising and deepening of religion. So the attention of the faithful was directed towards externals. Religion was materialised. Pious interest was focused more on the "holy things"—relics—than on the Sacraments, more on pilgrimages and flagellations than on attending the services of the Church, and most of all on indulgences.

The cult of relics and indulgences had grown to gigantic proportions since Leo X had attached indulgences of a thousand, ten thousand and a hundred thousand years to the veneration of relics. Erasmus criticised this kind of piety in the bitter words "We kiss the shoes of the saints and their dirty kerchiefs while we leave their writings, their holiest and truest relics, to lie unread" (Lortz I, 108). Frederick the Wise, the famous protector of Luther, had built up his treasury of relics in the Castle Church at Wittenburg to 18,885 fragments. Anyone who believed in and venerated them could gain indulgences amounting to two million years. When Boniface IX made of ecclesiastical indulgences what looked like a commercial traffic even secular princes and cities became eager to take part in the distribution of them, so as to assure for themselves a generous share of the inflowing money.[1]

From the middle of the fifteenth century the Popes began to distribute indulgences for the dead. The Legate Peraudi, in connection with an indulgence granted by Pope Sixtus IV to Louis XI for the whole of France, announces that the indulgence could be made *certainly* effective for any soul in Purgatory, even if the person gaining it was in a state of mortal sin, so long as the indulgenced work (i.e., money payment) was performed. Pope Sixtus IV did indeed correct his Legate's declaration to the extent of saying that the application of the indulgence to the dead could only be a matter of *petition*, not of certainty. But Peraudi's other statement—that the indulgence could be gained for the dead by people living in mortal sin—

---

[1] The Jubilee Indulgence of 1390 was extended to various cities besides Rome. A condition for gaining it was a money payment, collected by bankers appointed in the different towns who retained half the sum collected as a commission. See Vansteenberghe, article "Boniface IX" in the *Dictionnaire d' histoire et de géographie ecclesiastique*, vol. IX (1937), p. 919. (Trans.)

was never censured. In the prevailing low state of clerical education, preachers of the indulgence (such as the Dominican Tetzel for instance) eagerly seized on Peraudi's pronouncement, so that many preachers really did adopt as their favourite tag "Your cash no sooner clinks in the bowl than out of Purgatory jumps the soul". Some of the papal decrees themselves were in great measure responsible for this crude interpretation of indulgences. They employed a misleading formula current from the thirteenth century onwards which spoke of a *remissio a poena et culpa* (remission of pain and guilt) or even of a *remissio peccatorum* (remission of sins),[1] whereas an indulgence is not concerned with the forgiveness of the guilt of sin, nor with the remission of eternal punishment, but only with the remission of temporal punishment, that is, a mitigation or shortening of that penitential suffering which the sinner must undergo either here or in Purgatory.

It is unnecessary to emphasise how much this hideous simoniacal abuse of indulgences corrupted true piety, and how indulgences were perverted to a blasphemous haggling with God. Night fell on the German Church, a night that grew ever deeper and darker as other abuses attached themselves to the excessive cult of relics and the practice of indulgences. The latter was encouraged by the current mass-pilgrimages which were positively epidemic. Associated with them, especially at the time of the Great Schism, was the movement of the flagellants, in which pilgrimage was combined with public self-scourging. Though condemned alike by Pope Clement VI and the Council of Constance they constantly reasserted themselves, uprooted the faithful from their proper situation

---

[1] These phrases were intended to refer, not only to the indulgence, but to the repentance and absolution that went before it as well. But from the jubilee of 1390 onwards confessors and preachers of indulgences often failed entirely to refer to the necessity of repentance. See Vansteenberghe, loc. cit. (Trans.)

in parochial and domestic life, and threw them into a state of hysterical excess and unhealthy mysticism.

Behind all these excesses was the driving power of rampant superstition. Allying itself with religion, it had taken possession of the broad mass of the people. It is probably true to say that this superstition had made itself even more at home in the German soul than elsewhere, and developed, even amongst educated people, a vast obsession with the devil. It was a lingering heritage from Germanic and Roman paganism. Since the Inquisition's campaign against the Catharists, who had acknowledged Evil as a first principle, this devil-obsession had begun to ruin daily living and social intercourse. In particular was a totally uncritical acceptance of every kind of unprobable horror charged against witches. The witch-trials and witch-burnings went on—by inquisitors, secular governments, the reformers (Luther himself taught that witches must be destroyed): and the official Church did not shield the victims of these atrocities with the bulwark of clear Gospel teaching. On the contrary, Innocent VIII, in his Bull *Summis desiderantes* 1484, gave the Dominicans in Constance plenary powers in the matter of witch-burning, and threatened with ecclesiastical punishments anyone who opposed the prosecution of witches. He thus did all that the highest ecclesiastical authority could do to encourage and legalise the obsession. Christ had healed those possessed by devils, but now, in the name of the same Christ, they were to be burnt.

It was night indeed in a great part of Christendom. Such is the conclusion of our survey of the end of the fifteenth century: amongst the common people, a fearful decline of true piety into religious materialism and morbid hysteria; amongst the clergy, both lower and higher, widespread worldliness and neglect of duty; and amongst the very Shepherds of the

Church, demonic ambition and sacrilegious perversion of holy things. Both clergy and people must cry *mea culpa, mea maxima culpa!*

Yes, it was night. Had Martin Luther then arisen with his marvellous gifts of mind and heart, his warm penetration of the essence of Christianity, his passionate defiance of all unholiness and ungodliness, the elemental fury of his religious experience, his surging, soul-shattering power of speech, and not least that heroism in the face of death with which he defied the powers of this world—had he brought all these magnificent qualities to the removal of the abuses of the time and the cleansing of God's garden from weeds, had he remained a faithful member of his Church, humble and simple, sincere and pure, then indeed we should to-day be his grateful debtors. He would be forever our great Reformer, our true man of God, our teacher and leader, comparable to Thomas Aquinas and Francis of Assisi. He would have been the greatest saint of our people, the refounder of the Church in Germany, a second Boniface . . .

But—and here lies the tragedy of the Reformation and of German Christianity—he let the warring spirits drive him to overthrow not merely the abuses in the Church, but the Church Herself, founded upon Peter, bearing through the centuries the *successio apostolica*; he let them drive him to commit what St. Augustine calls the greatest sin with which a Christian can burden himself: he set up altar against altar and tore in pieces the one Body of Christ.

How did this come about? And must we continue for ever to join in that lament of contemporary Christendom which St. Augustine sounded in his work against the Donatists, *Ego laceror valde* (cruelly am I torn)? These are questions which I shall seek to answer in the next lecture.

II

HOW LUTHER LEFT THE CHURCH

THE POSSIBILITY OF REUNION

WHEN WE pass in review the abuses in the government and people of the Church described in the previous lecture, the conviction is borne in upon us that everything points to an imminent storm. The angry clamour for a reform in Head and members could be silenced no longer. But to speak of a *reform of the Head* was an unmistakable indication that people in Germany were not thinking of discarding the Head of the Church, but of improving him. Apart from a few groups of radical humanists and sectarians, the universal detestation was not for the Pope as the divinely instituted guarantee of the Church's unity, not for the religious authority of the Papal See, but only for the utter worldliness of the Popes and the Curia. The desire of all was to have at Rome a real representative of Christ, breathing the spirit of Christ in his person and activity. And when speaking of a reform of the members, no one thought for a moment of revolutionary changes in the nature of the Church. There was no desire to alter the substance of dogma, cult or ecclesiastical government, only to abolish all the obvious aberrations and distortions of the Church's inner life and devotion. If we avoid being distracted by merely incidental phenomena, and fix our attention on the whole climate of opinion which determined the spirit of the time, we see that the cry for reform was not anti-papal in any dogmatic sense, nor anti-ecclesiastical. It was a simple, elementary cry for conversion, for total renewal. The conviction had penetrated to the lowest levels of the Christian community that this state of affairs could not go on, that the very heart of the Church was disordered, that, one way or another, a re-formation must come. One way or another! As soon as the possibility was admitted that the change might come some *other* way than that which loyalty to the Church would demand, rebellious and threatening voices mingled with the chorus of the reformers, voices which announced, in the manner of Joachim of Flora, the approach of an apocalyptic visitation and the violent overthrow of all things.

But all these voices went unheard. The Lateran Council of 1513 might energetically deplore the evil state of the Church in Head and members, but a really effective will to reform was lacking. In the next body of Cardinals to be created, those who were to be confronted by the Lutheran movement, it was still the prince-prelates of the Renaissance who dominated the picture (Lortz I, 193), not determined men of reforming spirit. And amongst the Popes of the succeeding period, except for Adrian VI, from Clement VII until we arrive at Pius V, there was not one who seriously considered a reform in Head and members. What followed was therefore inevitable. Instead of a reform there was a revolution, a radical change in the fundamental substance of the Church and Christianity.

The man who kindled the revolution and pushed on relentlessly towards a final break with the Church was Martin Luther. He was not merely the creator and head of the new movement. He *was* that movement. For that which the Protestant confessions of to-day have in common—what we call to-day the "material principle" of Protestantism, its dogma of the exclusive activity of God and salvation by faith alone, and what we call its "formal principle", its acknowledgment of no other authority than that of Holy Writ—grew out of Luther's whole personal experience and is in its deepest origins his own personal invention. However much Luther may have resisted the dubbing of his own followers "Lutherans", Protestantism is nevertheless in its fundamental substance Lutheran through and through, Luther himself extended and developed.

How did Luther arrive at his new Gospel?

Considering as we are the possibility of a reunion of the Christian confessions, it is extremely important to affirm, along with all modern research on the subject of Luther, that the abuses in the Church outlined in the first lecture were not the real *cause* but only the *occasion* of the Reformation. These abuses, and their culmination in the shameful deal in indulgences between the Hohenzollern Prince Albert of Brandenburg, the Archbishop of Magdeburg and Mainz and the Papal Curia,[1] undoubtedly aroused Luther to the point of coming forward publicly. They explain too why it was that the theses he nailed to the door of the Castle Church at Wittenburg, *De virtute indulgentiarum* (concerning the power of indulgences), unleashed such tremendous forces in the German people. Most important of all, they made it possible for Luther to put the Church in the wrong and to justify his own doctrine as the

---

[1] The preaching of the special Indulgence for the building of St. Peter's was allowed by the Archbishop of Magdeburg and Mainz in his dioceses only on condition that the net profit was to be halved between himself and the fund for St. Peter's. The Archbishop made an arrangement with the great German banking family, the Fuggers, whereby they collected the money. He thus repaid them the sums advanced to him to cover his fees to the Curia for his appointment to the See of Mainz and for the privilege of retaining the Sees of Halberstadt and Magdeburg contrary to Canon Law. See Philip Hughes, *History of the Church*, vol. III, pp. 501-2. (Trans.)

one gospel of salvation before the mass of the people and before his own conscience. Indeed, the longer the strife continued, the more violent became the clash of spirits, the more passionately Luther's hatred of the Pope's Church flamed up; and as he grew older, the confusion in his eyes between the abuses in the Church and the essence of the Church increased, his belief in himself and his mission deepened, and he developed an ever more convinced and more triumphant assurance that he was being summoned by God to overthrow Antichrist in the shape of the Pope.

Thus the abuses within the mediaeval Church certainly unleashed Luther upon the path of revolution, and justified him in the eyes of the masses and in his own judgment. But they were not the actual ground, the decisive reason for Luther's falling away from the doctrine of the Church. He himself, even, later emphasised that one should not condemn a man's teaching "merely because of his sinful life". "That is not the Holy Spirit. For the Holy Spirit condemns false doctrine and is patient with the weak in faith, as is taught in Romans xiv. 15, and everywhere in Paul. I would have little against the Papists if they taught true doctrine. Their evil life would do no great harm" (Lortz I, 390). It was not ecclesiastical abuses that made him the opponent of the Catholic Church, but the conviction that she was *teaching* falsely. And this conviction dates from long before the fatal 17th October, 1517. He had interiorly abandoned the teaching of the Church long before he outwardly raised the standard of revolt. Certainly as early as 1512, without as yet knowing or wishing it, he had grown away from the Church's belief (Lortz I, 191). How did this come about? In asking this question, we are confronted by the mystery of Luther, by the problem of his whole personal development.

In reaching a judgment on his development it is necessary to remember that Luther, doubtless very strictly brought up in his father's house at Eisleben, was early imbued with a strong central experience of fear, an extraordinary terror of sin and judgment. This alone accounts for the fact that when he was caught in a thunderstorm near Stotternheim and nearly struck by lightning he cried out, "Help me, Saint Anne! I will become a monk." He was overcome by a similar spiritual crisis at his first Mass. It was so violent that he almost had to leave the celebration unfinished. It is also significant that once, when at the conventual Mass the Gospel of the man possessed by the devil was being read, he cried out, "It is not I!" and fell down like a dead man (Lortz I, 161, note). These accesses of terror betray an unusual degree of sensitivity, stimulated by his deeply rooted fear in the face of the *tremendum mysterium* of God, which for him reached its most shattering clarity in the Crucifixion of the Son of God. Since his attitude to life was determined at its very roots by this fear, Luther was radically subjectivist. That is to say, he was naturally inclined to take into the tension of his own subjective consciousness all objective truths and values presented to him from without, and only then to evaluate their importance and significance. If any truth or value could not be thus assimilated to the thoughts already in the depths of his fearful soul, he had no great interest in it. Thus his religious thought was from the start eclectic, one-sidedly selective. From the start it was thought overcharged with feeling, enveloped by a secret fear and labouring under the tormenting question: how am I to find a merciful God? From the start the primary object of his thought was to release the tension in his own soul, to deliver himself, to bring tranquillity to his distraught spirit. Always the stress was on *I*, everything pivoting on his own experience. On the other hand, it cannot

c

be doubted, in face of Luther's tremendous achievements in thought, decision and action, that despite this tension he was psychically healthy to the core. In everything that he thought, preached and wrote Luther betrays a robust vitality, an over-flowing energy, an inexhaustible originality, an elemental creative power which raised him far above the level of common humanity.

With these predispositions, Luther entered the Priory of barefooted Augustinians at Erfurt, probably against his father's will. Here he was to prepare himself, by strict spiritual discipline and hard study, for his future entry into the Order and the priesthood. The system of thought, the form in which all philosophical knowledge was then presented, both in the priory and in the neighbouring University of Wittenberg, was the *Via moderna* of Scotism, with the stamp of its later Ockham-ist development. Ockhamism had a decisive influence on Luther. He described himself as a member of the Ockhamist school (*sum occamicae factionis*). More precisely, he counted himself a Gabrielist, i.e., a follower of the Tübingen theologian Gabriel Biel, who had adapted Ockhamism, bringing it more into line with the teaching of the Church.

From Ockhamism Luther received his anti-metaphysical tendencies, his dislike of the Aristotelian and Scholastic doc-trine founded on the objective validity of universal concepts. From Ockham too he took his concept of God. God is God precisely because of His absolute, unconditioned Will, His sovereign freedom and dominion, which is beyond any scale of values and by Whose arbitrary choice alone this order of values was created. God is a God of arbitrary choice. He can therefore predestine some in advance to eternal salvation, others in advance to eternal damnation.

Particularly important for Luther's inner development is the

Ockhamist doctrine of justification. Pre-Lutheran Thomism, the Church's classical doctrine of grace, presents grace as a movement of divine love entering into the penitent soul and delivering it from the bonds of its fallen nature. In contrast with this, grace in Ockhamism remains strictly transcendent. Justification consists solely in a *relatio externa*, a new relationship of mercy between man and God established by God's love, by means of which all a man's religious and moral acts, *though remaining in themselves human and natural*, are accounted as salvific acts in the eyes of a merciful God. In Ockhamism, it is true, justification is still God's work of grace, in so far as human activity only becomes salvific by God's recognition of it, by His act of acceptance. But this recognition and validation does not in any way affect man's spiritual powers. It remains completely outside him and is simply seen and assented to by faith. Thus for practical purposes on the psychological plane it is as though nothing were involved but purely human activity, and as if devotion were only a matter of human acts.

Thus the intellectual situation in which Luther found himself was insecure and threatened on all sides. Natural reality was not a harmony of truths and values, accessible to knowledge and fundamentally intelligible, but an ultimately unknowable multiplicity of concrete singulars, a world of confusion and riddles. And supernatural reality, the living God of revelation, is a hidden God (*deus absconditus*), far removed from any kind of tie, sheer creative omnipotence to which we are completely delivered up. There is but one way of escape from this overwhelming combined threat from above and below: blind fulfilment of the arbitrary commands of this arbitrary God as they are shown to us in Revelation, the way of good works. It is a way crowded at each moment with moral activity, but for this very reason a perilous way, a way of stumbling and falling.

It is easy to see that the perilous and menacing situation thus resulting from the ideas of Ockhamism was bound to have a seriously disturbing effect on a religious sensibility already as troubled with fear as Luther's. The consequence was a series of crises, struggles and temptations. The readings from the Bible and from the writings of St. Augustine upon which his Order laid particular stress again helped to increase Luther's religious terror. It was in fact St. Augustine who, in his disputes with the Semi-Pelagians, pushed the Biblical doctrine of predestination to the furthest extreme, going so far as to speak of a "reprobate mass" from which only a few just would be chosen. Luther's first years in the Priory were thus a time of interior tension, spiritual struggle and suffering. The hopeless feeling that he was not numbered among the elect but among the reprobate overcame him and grew stronger as he grew more and more conscious that he did not fulfil God's commandments in all things. Since he began early to condemn as sin every movement of natural appetite, even though unwilling, and since, with his exuberant vitality, such movements kept recurring, he supposed himself to be full of sin, and no prayer, fasting or confession could free him from this terror.

For many years Luther was thus visited by scruples. "I know a man who believes that he has often experienced the pains of Hell" (Lortz I, 174), a sign of the seriousness with which he regarded his vocation as a Christian and a religious, and on the other hand an indication of how far Ockhamism had obscured the Christian gospel of grace. The strange and tragic thing in Luther's development was that, in his Ockhamist aversion from all metaphysics and especially from the *via antiqua* of Scholasticism, he remained closed to the traditional Catholic doctrine of grace as represented by the great masters of Scholasticism, Albert the Great, Thomas Aquinas and Bonaventure. It suffered indeed a temporary decline in the late Middle Ages, but was taken up again by the *princeps Thomistarum* Johannes Capreolus and re-established in all its ancient purity by Luther's contemporary, Cardinal Cajetan. Ockhamist optimism, in fact, in its practical, living results, bordered close on the Pelagian denial of Original Sin. In contrast to this the Catholic teaching sets the *homo lapsus*, man burdened with Original Sin and its consequences, in the centre of the divine plan of salvation. It does not present salvation as a pronouncement by God's free graciousness of the justice of our purely human efforts to teach the redemptive riches of Christ. Salvation consists on the contrary in the grace and love of Christ, merited by the sacrifice of the Cross and penetrating fallen man, constantly washing away our guilt and supplying for our weakness by the Sacraments and awakening us to new life in Christ. The fundamental attitude of redeemed man, according to the Church's doctrine, is thus not the fear of sin and terror of damnation but trusting faith in the grace of Christ, which constantly snatches us away from all guilt and gives us Christ for our own. If Luther had entrusted himself to this traditional Catholic doctrine of Grace, which his friend Johann von Staupitz, the Augustinian Provincial, constantly laid before him, he would not have had that experience in the tower which laid the foundation for his abandonment of the doctrine of the Church.

Luther describes this experience in 1545, one year before his death—fairly late, in fact. His other recollections were also made late in life, and contain a number of "foreshortenings" of various kinds (Lortz I, 178). So it is likely enough that a whole series of thoughts and impressions of a similar kindled up

to this decisive experience in the monastery tower at Wittenburg, which was merely the final precipitation of them. In
any case, a fundamental departure from the Catholic doctrine
of justification is settled once for all in this experience in the
tower in 1512. As Luther himself expressed it, it was concerned with a deeper understanding of the Epistle to the
Romans, starting with the Pauline concept of the "justice of
God". St. Paul had written "The justice of God is revealed
therein"—i.e., in the Gospel (Rom. i. 17). Hitherto he had
not been able to make anything of the scriptural words "the
justice of God". "I did not love this just God, the punisher of
sins, rather I hated him." Only after pondering a long while
"both day and night" did he perceive that the Apostle of the
Gentiles did not mean by the "justice of God" active, judicial,
primitive justice, but passive justice, i.e., that by which the
merciful God justifies us by faith, as it is written: "The just
man liveth by faith." Luther immediately re-examined in this
light all the related texts in Holy Scripture which he remembered at the time, and found that they were all to be understood in this sense. "Then truly I felt that I had been born
again and had entered through open gates into the highest
heaven."

Thus his experience in the tower laid the foundation of
Luther's *theology of consolation*: Christianity is pure grace, not
the work of man. It is in this sense that he interprets the words
of the Apostle (Rom. iii. 28): "For we account a man to be
justified by faith, without the works of the law." It is strange
that Luther should have considered that this interpretation of
the "justice of God" was a completely *new* discovery, differen-
tiating his exegesis from that of "all the doctors". In actual
fact practically all the mediaeval exegetes proposed the same
meaning for it. They all took "the justice of God" in the

passive sense, as meaning a justice by which we are justified, which makes us just. But they did not draw from this the catastrophic conclusion that Luther drew and which, in his 1515–16 lectures on the Epistle to the Romans, he claimed as the true meaning and content of the Epistle: "In the Epistle to the Romans Paul teaches us the reality of sin in us and the unique justice of Christ." This is the culminating point of his new discovery: man is sin, nothing but sin. Even the man who is justified remains *peccator*. What justifies him is the sole justice of Christ, imputed to him on the ground of his trusting faith. There is thus no question of the justice of any work of man. Man's part is merely to recognise his sinfulness in true repentance and, in this terror-stricken awareness (*conscientia pavida*), to reach out towards the Cross of Christ. It is God's grace alone which delivers him. As Christ Himself was at once "accursed and blessed", living and dead, suffering and rejoicing, so the believing Christian is at once a sinner and justified. From now on Luther delights in thus putting the inexpressible in the form of a paradox: the believing Christian is at once a sinner and justified, at once condemned and absolved, at once accursed and blessed.

From the psychological point of view, Luther's total denial of any justice in works and his unconditional assent to grace alone constituted an act of self-liberation from the fearful oppression which his moral life had suffered under Ockhamist theology and its exclusive emphasis on the human factor in the process of justification. From now on he resolutely cast himself loose from *all* justice in works, from all human activity, and threw himself upon the justifying grace of Christ, thus getting rid once and for all of all scrupulosity and terror of sin. Now he is spiritually free: free not only from the exaggerations of the Ockhamist School with its over-emphasis on works, but free from *any* form of justice in works, including that which the Catholic Church had always taught; free, as he was later to say, from the *captivitas babylonica*.

He won this freedom through a series of arduous battles and defeats, in hard struggles by day and night. It is this that gives his new experience its inner validity and its tremendous explosive power. If he had attained to this new interpretation of justification by a purely speculative process, as a mere intellectual conclusion, an exegetical discovery, the matter might have rested there. He might have remained unmolested within the Church, since there were other Catholic theologians, of the Augustinian school, teaching something similar, and since no Tridentine dogma had yet authoritatively defined the relation between faith and works, or the process of justification. His new theses would perhaps have been attacked here and there, perhaps have been censured. He might have been regarded as a theological outsider, but he would still have remained a Catholic theologian. But his expositions were more than mere academic treatises; for him, those ninety-five theses nailed to the door of the Castle Church at Wittenberg mirrored the *Evangelium*, the sole hope of salvation, upon which one could stake one's life; and the source of this feeling is to be found in those nights in the monastery, those hours of fear and agony when he burned with the fierce heat of his struggles for his soul's salvation. His new interpretation of the justice of God was sealed with his heart's blood, born of the dire need of his conscience—and for this reason it was infinitely dear to him. All the defiance of his passionate temperament, all the unrepressed impetuosity of his robust peasant nature, the rich endowments of his mind, his heroic readiness to commit himself to the full, his immense creative power in observation, thought and writing, and not least his wonderful power of speech, beating upon the hearer in climax after climax and "fairly overwhelming him" (Lortz I, 147)—all these powers united now in a tremendous *sense of mission*, a conviction that he, he alone, had rediscovered the Gospel and was called to proclaim it to the whole world. Armed with this sense of mission, which asserted itself ever more strongly and triumphantly as the years went by, he, the barefoot Augustinian friar of Wittenberg, went forth against a whole world, against the Christian Middle Ages, against the weight of the worldwide Catholic Church, against Pope and Emperor, and, not the least formidable, against the bronze ring of sacred custom with which men's consciences had for centuries been inextricably bound.

Let me stress it once again: Luther's abandonment of belief in the Church was not a conclusion reached in the cold, clear light of critical thought, but in the heat of religious experience; indeed, his whole development was less a matter of intellectual insights than of emotional impressions. From the sheer intellectual point of view, Luther *never* abandoned the idea of the one true Church. His theological *thought* did not touch on the erection of a new Church, but on the renewal of the old. Even in 1518, when he had to give an account of himself to the Cardinal-Legate Cajetan, he declared: "If any man can show me that I have said anything contrary to the opinion of the holy Roman Church, I will be my own judge, and recant" (Lortz I, 393). And in the *Commentary on a certain Article* in 1519 he commits himself, entirely according to the mind of St. Augustine, to the principle that one may not "for any sin or evil whatever that man may think or name, sever love and divide spiritual unity, for love can do all things."

But the world of feeling within him had been stirred to its depths; the violence of his experience overwhelmed all these rational considerations. The harder his Catholic opponents pressed him, the more he let himself be swept into a declaration of war against the whole Church. In his ninety-five theses on indulgences he had already questioned the power of the Church over the riches of salvation; in his Leipzig Disputation in 1519 he attacked the infallible authority of General Councils and of the Church's doctrinal tradition and admitted as religious truth only what can be deduced from Holy Scripture. From 1520 onwards he openly attacked the Pope as Antichrist. His address, *To the Christian Nobility of the German Nation*, which appeared in the same year, was, as Karl Müller expresses it, "a trumpet-call to seize all the possessions of the Papacy". And in his later polemical writing, *De Captivitate Babylonica*, of the Church's seven Sacraments he admitted only Baptism, the Lord's Supper, and, partially, Penance, branding the other Sacraments, together with the Church's teaching on Transubstantiation and the Sacrifice of the Mass, as *captivitas babylonica*, a miserable imprisonment of the faithful. In the work which was the third main statement of the Reformation, *Of the Freedom of a Christian Man*, he portrayed the ideal of Christian life in the light of his new doctrine and sent it to the Pope. In this same year 1520, as the public expression of his complete abandonment of the Church, he burned the volumes of the Canon Law and the Papal Bull threatening him with excommunication before the Elster Gate of Wittenberg. The Pope's answer was sentence of excommunication.

His break with the Church was complete. He went forward in the midst of a mass-apostasy of princes and cities, secular and regular clergy, nobles and humanists, burghers and peasants. There followed the Protestation of the Lutheran Princes and Cities against the decision of the Reichstag at Speier in 1529, which gave the new religionists the name of

"Protestants". And then came the Reichstag at Augsburg in 1530, which, with its rejection of Melanchthon's mediatory *Confessio Augustana*, destroyed the last hope of a reconciliation of minds. Christianity in Germany was divided, and has remained so until this very day.

Is Reunion Possible?

We come now to our second question: is a reunion between the divided Churches actually *possible*? To put the question more precisely: are not the ideas which distinguish the Christian Confessions actually opposed to one another rather than merely divergent, so that any understanding or agreement is out of the question from the start? Or does a closer view rather show that both Churches have much in common, and even that the beliefs which differentiate them come together, ultimately, in the fundamental basis which is common to both religions?

We must first reiterate the fact, admitted by all modern scholars, that Luther's departure from the Church's rule of faith was brought about by a *subjective* experience—his experience in the tower in 1512. As we have already said, abuses in the Church certainly strengthened Luther in this experience. They certainly armed him with his best weapons against Rome, and accounted to no small extent for the tremendous response of the German nation to his new Gospel. But they did not create this Gospel; Luther did not arrive at his new interpretation of the Gospel by looking at the deplorable abuses in the Church around him. He arrived at it by looking at the crying need of his own soul, the result of the conflict between the terror of sin which had oppressed him from his youth and the rigorous demands made on him by the

Ockhamist doctrine of atonement. He was delivered from these straits by his experience of all-sufficient saving faith, the experience of grace alone. It was a completely subjective experience arising out of the acute anxiety of his own individual mind, and it was so elemental in character that it not only drew into itself all similar religious impressions and dominated them, but also spread out over all his thinking and compelled him to see and accept only those truths which came in some way within the orbit of this central experience, and to ignore all the truths of Scripture which lay outside it. Only thus can we explain, for instance, his calling the Epistle of St. James, because of its emphasis on the justice of works, an "epistle of straw". Only thus can we explain the fact that he does not go in the first instance to Christ our Lord Himself, speaking to us in the Gospels, but to the written testimony of St. Paul, the last of the Apostles to be called, who was never an eye- or ear-witness of the life of Jesus. And only thus can we explain his complete failure to realise what interpolations and re-arrangements need to be made to derive that doctrine of grace which Luther thought he could find in St. Paul from the most profound passages of Jesus' own teaching, the Sermon on the Mount, with its clear theme of works and rewards.

The subjectivity of his central experience can be said to have dominated his theology, determining the special way in which he read and commented the Bible. It is a theology of subjective selection. Luther was certainly not a religious individualist in the ordinary sense, trusting exclusively to the emanations of his own thought and to his own experiences when dealing with theological issues. On the contrary, his trembling spirit was confronted by the colossal reality of the God of Revelation, and the shattering impact of His Gospel. He knew himself bound to this mightiest of objectivities, in the same way that he continued to accept ancient and mediaeval cosmology as final truth. To this extent Luther was, as Troeltsch puts it (*Collected Writings*, 1922, IV, p. 286), "a completely conservative revolutionary". The word of Revelation laid down in the Bible remained for him the unique source of all religious knowledge. But it was not the objective spirit of the Church's tradition speaking and witnessing in the Church's teaching which interpreted this objective word of Revelation, but his *own* spirit alone; not the *We* of the members of Christ inspired by a common faith and love, but his own unique, individual *I*. In this formal, though not material, sense Luther was always a subjectivist.

It is true that this subjectivism arose largely from truly religious depths, rooted, ultimately, in an elementary experience of the uncertainty and the helpless need for salvation of fallen human nature. There could be no greater mistake than to see, in the religious movement which had Luther as its origin, nothing but the product of a completely personal fear-psychosis. Luther's fear is the fear of all of us, the guilty fear of human nature enmeshed in the consequences of Original Sin. This alone explains why the Reformer's experience was, and is, capable of creating a communion. But on the other hand, neither can it be doubted that the special structure of this experience, its depth and comprehensiveness and its theological and sociological developments, bear always those marks of subjectivism which belong to Luther's singular, exceptional spiritual development alone, and are in no way common to humanity.

"Luther's great mistake in constituting his doctrine was that he took his own highly personal convictions, based on a very exceptional experience and perhaps valid for himself personally, and made them into a binding requirement for all."

(Lortz I, 408). It was to be expected from the start that this subjectivist basis would be far too narrow and scanty to remain the standard interpretation of Christ for a whole world with its thousands of individual characters. Thus even in Luther's own lifetime divisions arose over essential points. Before his very eyes there took place a certain loosening and weakening of his doctrine, a loosening which left open at least the *possibility* that even the most differing sects might be able to meet each other in discussion.

The scholarly side of Lutheran Christianity, as much as its individual and even individualist origin, offers many things favourable to an understanding with Catholic Christianity. We must, of course, make it clear first that we are not considering the emasculated Christianity produced by the Enlightenment and German Idealist philosophy but *Luther's* Christianity, the original Lutheranism which he himself founded and built up. In a stimulating lecture entitled *What are Catholic Tendencies?* a leading Lutheran Bishop, Wilhelm Stählin of Oldenburg, has made a determined attack on that modern perversion of Lutheran belief which considers the "banalities of unbridled liberalism" born of the Enlightenment as the true essence of Protestantism. It is an attitude which thinks that the difference between Protestant and Catholic is simply that the Protestant "feels that he is only responsible to his own conscience", so that for him there is "no binding dogma and no compulsory creed", or at any rate, that he "pushes certain aspects of the Bible message out of sight or at least to the very edge of his field of vision". Anyone who speaks of the binding nature of a dogma, of the presence of Christ in the cult of the Church or of a necessary ecclesiastical order is at once—so Stählin complains—accused of Catholic tendencies. In fact, he says with emphasis, dogma, cult and the Church's constitution belong to the *"true heritage* of the Reformation". And in reality it was "a sign of decline, a morbid symptom" when these ordinances were set aside in the name of the individual conscience. "If a man believes," Stählin goes on to say, "that he can sacrifice the fullness of the Christian revelation to some vague formless religious feeling or vague belief in Providence, he may hold himself to be a good Protestant, but in the true Reformation sense of the word, he is simply not a Christian."

To some extent this condemnation of Stählin's falls also on a type of Lutheran theology and a mental attitude which regards the liberation of the individual's conscience from despair as the essence of Christianity, and entirely ignores the sacramental *framework* in which this conscience has its roots, the holy ordinances of the Church. Of such a Protestantism it is true to say what Nietzsche believed to be true of Protestantism in general—that it was "a one-sided laming" of Christianity (*Antichrist* VIII, 225).

Luther himself did not leave the matter in doubt; for him the Confession of Augsburg in 1530 was compulsory doctrine, acknowledgment of which was a condition of membership of the Church (cf. Loofs, *History of Dogma*, 4th ed. p. 748). So we are confronted, in Lutheran Christianity, with the recognition of an *objective ecclesiastical teaching authority*, with which every individual Christian conscience must come to terms. It is true that the Protestant conscience is more loosely bound to this authority than a Catholic's is, because the authority does not, as in the Catholic Church, rest upon the visible rock of Peter and is not visibly guaranteed by the apostolic succession of Bishops. Looking at it closely, the Protestant conscience is bound to the collective mind of the Church as a whole, not to those visible authorities in particular who are the bearers and sustainers of that collective mind. Nevertheless, in Lutheranism too, Christian consciences are not simply sovereign, but obliged to submit to the teaching voice of their Church.

Indeed we might go further, and say that though Protestant consciences may be more loosely bound, the tie is not *essentially* any different from that binding the Catholic. For the Catholic, too, it is not ultimately the objective norm of the teaching voice but the subjective decision of *conscience* which has finally to decide on a believing acceptance of the revealed truth laid down by the authority of the Church. It is really not the case that the faith of a Catholic is entirely accounted for by slavish obedience to the rigid law of the Church. He, too, is making a personal act, an act of reflective thought and moral decision springing from the deep centre of his freedom, an act of choice. For him too it is an act that can only be performed in the conscience itself. Indeed, if his conscience, on subjectively cogent grounds, becomes involved in invincible error and he finds himself compelled to refuse his assent to the Church's teaching, he is, in the Catholic view, bound to leave the Church. The most eminent of Catholic theologians, St. Thomas Aquinas, expressly declares that a man is bound in conscience to separate himself from the Christian body if he is unable to believe in the divinity of Christ.[1] Thus the two confessions meet each other both in their recognition of an ecclesiastical teaching authority and in the decisive place they give to the judgment of the individual conscience.

Furthermore, in their attitude to the Sacred Scriptures they are not nearly so opposed to each other as might appear from the formal Lutheran principle of "the Scripture alone". The Catholic Church re-affirmed and reformulated in the Councils

[1] *Summa Theologica* I–II, 19. 5.

of Trent and of the Vatican the ancient truth of the Christian faith that Scripture is inspired by the Holy Ghost, whereas modern Protestant theology tends more and more to admit only Revelation, not Scripture, as inspired, the bearers of the Revelation being themselves enlightened by the Holy Ghost, but not their writings. So that one can say that the authority of Holy Scripture is fundamentally better safeguarded and more strongly emphasised in Catholicism than in Protestantism.

Because they are inspired by the Holy Ghost, the Scriptures, and especially the New Testament, are always, for the Catholic too, the classical source of Christianity. They present, so to speak, the conscious mind of the Church. But the Catholic is convinced that the Church has also what might be called a subconscious mind. It consists of those remembrances, ordinances and traditions of primitive Christianity received directly from Christ but handed on only *orally* by the Apostles, which were not expressly formulated in Holy Scripture, although in the strictest sense they embody a primitive Christian deposit of faith. This extra-Biblical stream of tradition must have existed from the beginning, since the first disciples, like their Divine Master, at first spread the Good News only orally, and it was by oral teaching alone that they aroused the faith of the first Christian communities. When they wrote the Gospels and Epistles, they already took for granted the existence of a living Christianity in the various communities, as the writings themselves show.

Nor is it of course the case that the Apostles and Evangelists were trying to achieve in their writings a comprehensive, exhaustive survey of the Christian message, a sort of early catechism. It would be hard even to-day to piece together a single, unselfcontradictory system of thought from the Bible

D

without reference to the oral tradition. The aim of the Apostles and Evangelists was rather to *inspire* and *deepen* the religion of the Christian communities, always according to the different circumstances in which they wrote and with reference to the growing problems which they encountered—not in any true sense to *establish* it. Thus not all the Apostles wrote; and again several of St. Paul's epistles are lost to us. What brought the Christian communities to life in the first place was *oral preaching*, not the Scriptures. Again, we only know of the very existence of the Scriptures, and of what is included in them, by oral tradition. To this extent their authority is ultimately dependent upon that of the Church's teaching.

In the light of this overwhelming importance attaching to the Church's tradition, the Lutheran scriptural principle cannot any longer be upheld in its original form. On the other hand, we must remark on the Catholic side a re-awakening of interest in the Bible, which has not only affected professional theologians but has become a widespread movement among the common people of the Church. Nor is there any lack of voices acknowledging Luther's translation of the Bible, with its vigorous language tingling with the violence of religious experience, as a classical example worthy of emulation. Thus in our day a meeting ground on the question of the Bible is being developed between the Christian confessions which may produce rich results in mutual understanding.

We may look for even more fruitfulness from what we have in common in the *content* of belief.

It cannot be over-emphasised that those truths which are uniquely Christian, distinguishing Christianity from all other religions: the mysteries of the Three-Personed God, of the Son of God made man, of our redemption by the Cross, of the sanctification of the faithful by Baptism, Penance and Eucharist, of the coming of the Judge of all the world, of the Last Things —it is just this ground-plan and *centre* of the Christian message which forms the core of *both* our Christian confessions. Will it not be possible to find paths radiating from this centre which will bring us to unity in those things which are less central? What divides us is not so much *what* we believe as the various different ways in which we take into ourselves and realise this one gift of Faith—problems about the nature of saving faith, the process of justification, the relation between faith and sacrament, the teaching, pastoral and priestly office of the Church. These are certainly matters of importance, and, for the sake of revealed truth, we cannot neutralize them or indeed yield anything concerning them. But they are nevertheless questions which would not, in the light of *early* Lutheran piety, be so involved and utterly insoluble as would appear from the religious situation to-day.

We must consider, for example, the fact that Confession and the honouring of the Blessed Virgin—two forms of devotion which a modern Protestant condemns as specifically Catholic— occupied an important position in Luther's own devotional life. Right up to his death he paid homage in his sermons to the Mother of God; right up to his death he went to confession to his friend Bugenhagen. "I should long ago have been strangled by the Devil," he acknowledges, "if I had not been upheld by private confession." It was the orthodox Lutheran theology of the seventeenth and eighteenth centuries that eliminated devotion to Mary and Confession from Protestant practice.

We should be even more struck by the fact that the "Confession of Augsburg" (*Confessio Augustana*), drawn up by Melanchthon and approved by Luther, which in evangelical Christianity ranks even to-day as an authoritative confession of faith, makes no mention in its first part of any fundamental dogmatic difference, not even of the primacy of the Pope or Indulgences, and in fact expressly declares that the whole dispute is concerned only with certain *abuses* (*tota dissensio est de paucis quibusdam abusibus*). And in the second part, where it enumerates these abuses, it names simply: Communion under one kind, celibacy, private Masses (i.e., the current commercial traffic in hole-and-corner Masses), compulsory Confession, the laws of fasting, monastic vows and the abuse of episcopal authority; in other words, only things which in the Catholic view do not belong to the unalterable *regula fidei*, the sphere of faith, but to the *regula disciplinae*, the sphere of ecclesiastical discipline, which the Church could, if she saw fit, alter.

And even these abuses, as Melanchthon notes them, take on their repulsive, scandalous aspect only against the background of late mediaeval practice. We learnt in the first lecture how celibacy, monastic vows, compulsory confession and the so-called commercial hole-and-corner Masses had been perverted from the glorious truth that underlay them. These detestable perversions will never return. The reforming Council of Trent tore them up by the roots. The evangelical historian Karl August Meissinger made some significant remarks in this connection in his essay on "Luther's Day": "If Luther returned to-day . . . he would find to his astonishment a Roman Church which he would never have attacked in her present aspect . . . Above all he would see . . . that not one of the abuses which were the actual occasion of his break with Rome remains in existence."

It is true that Melanchthon, starting from his urgent wish for an understanding, seems to have been too optimistic when he spoke in the Confession simply of "certain abuses" which must be removed. For it cannot be doubted that Luther regarded some at least of his objections as fundamental. But here too we must not overlook the fact that in taking up this radical position he still started from the abuses within the Church, and that ultimately it was his total opposition, born of his deep religious experience, to everything unholy, together with his volcanic impetuosity, which led him to make a clean sweep, to be done completely with all these abuses, and then to provide his destructive beginnings with a theoretical basis.

We have already shown how even his principal doctrine of salvation by faith alone is largely accounted for by his resentment against the stress laid by Ockhamism on the human factor in justification. Since he was insufficiently acquainted with the great masters of Scholasticism, he simply identified the radically un-Catholic Ockhamist doctrine of justification with the teaching of the Catholic Church. When we look into it we see that his phrase "faith alone" is directly aimed only against the Ockhamist supposition that a man, once he is called to salvation by God's grace, can and must work out his own salvation by his own power and his own self-mastery. It was aimed, then, against the Pelagianism lurking in the Ockhamist doctrine of justification, which made salvation dependent solely on human power. But it was not directly aimed against that other supposition, that man can and must work out his salvation *by the power of Christ*, that all human choice and action only becomes salvific when it is caught up by the grace of Christ. It is a cleavage of ideas going right through to the heart of our conception of God: whether man is to be thought of as a completely autonomous, independent co-operator—or, if he wishes, opponent—of God in the scheme of redemption, or simply as passive in His hand, unable to work out his salvation except in grace and through grace. It is the latter which has always been the clear, unambiguous teaching of the Catholic Church. It was first actually formulated at the second Council of Orange in 529 against the Semi-Pelagians, and repeated at Trent, illuminated by our Lord's image of the branch which can only flourish and bring forth fruit in the vine. Looking at it truly and profoundly, it was not against *this* that Luther raged and fought. His doctrine of faith and grace alone would have had its right place, its true significance, within the framework of Catholic dogma, so long as he meant by "faith alone" that faith which is active through love.

In fact, the phrase "salvation by faith alone" has never been alien to Catholic theology. It was in fact always Catholic teaching that we can only be saved by Christ alone, that it is only God's unmerited, unmeritable grace that lifts us out of the state of sin and death into that of divine sonship, and that even the so-called "meritorious acts" which the redeemed perform in a state of justice are only "meritorious by grace", attributable, that is, to the love of Christ working in us and through us. In so far as the justification of man is God's work alone, we could speak with Luther of "extrinsic" justice. It is indeed also interior and personal. Luther too, in that same commentary on the Epistle to the Romans, affirms that this extrinsic justice "dwells in us by faith and hope", that it is "in us" though it does not belong to us (*in nobis est, non nostra*), that it thus, according to the Council of Trent, "inheres" in justified man (*atque ipsis inhaeret*, Trid, sess. 6, cap. 7, can. 11).

In the same way Luther's other doctrine, that the justified man is at once a sinner and just (*simul peccator et justus*), can bear a Catholic interpretation if we do not take it theologically but psychologically, if we regard justification not from God's point of view but from man's. In the first case it is indeed always a matter of Yes *or* No, election or reprobation, but in the second, it is a question of Yes *and* No, in so far as our hardest striving is always accompanied by some secret attachment to sin (cf. R. Grosche, *Pilgernde Kirche*, 1938, pp. 150 ff.). The Catholic too must pray day by day "forgive us our trespasses". Throughout his liturgy echoes the cry, "Lord, have mercy on us. Regard not my sins! Give us peace!" Even when the justified soul is no longer in a state of sin, it is still sinful. Every serious Catholic will wish and have to pray with St. Thérèse of the Child Jesus: ". . . I do not ask You to count my good works, Lord. All our justice is full of imperfection in Your eyes. So I will clothe myself in Your justice and receive from Your love eternal possession of Yourself."

It was the Thomistic School itself which anticipated Luther's pessimistic view of humanity, since it taught that the capacity of fallen man to receive God's action is purely passive, which grace alone can arouse to activity and freedom. We can affirm absolutely that Luther's battle, fundamentally and essentially, was only with the Ockhamist perversion of the Catholic doctrine of justification, with an abuse within the Church, as Melanchthon rightly saw, an abuse which was never accepted by the Church. Ockham himself was arraigned before a court of the Holy Office at Avignon[1] and kept in custody, until he fled to the protection of Ludwig of Bavaria; though the fact that the subsequent spread of his doctrine was tolerated gave the hot-blooded Reformer a seeming justification in identifying Ockhamism with Catholicism and in denying, along with the abuse itself, its primitive Christian and Catholic background.

A similar reaction against public abuses within the Church accounts for Luther's radical discarding of the seven Sacraments and the separate priesthood. In his polemic *De Captivate*

---

[1] But *not* for his teaching on justification. (Trans.)

Babylonica he expressly speaks of the multitude of human regulations with which the Church had made of the Sacraments a miserable captivity for the faithful.

His own master, Gabriel Biel, had taught him, entirely in accordance with the Catholic interpretation, that in the Mass there is no question of a fresh immolation of Christ, but only of a ritual re-presentation of the one sacrifice of Golgotha, and thus that through the Mass the one sacrifice of Christ is brought out of the past into our present moment, into our Here and Now. Nevertheless Luther's violent rejection of the sacrifice of the Mass can only be understood in relation to that crude externalisation, secularisation even, which had penetrated even to the innermost sanctuary of the Church and, as Luther complained, made "the Altar of the All Highest into an altar of Baal" (Lortz I, 399). When the clergy were not paid sufficiently for saying Mass they used to say a *missa sicca*, i.e., they broke off the Mass before the Consecration. And when the faithful had a Mass said for them they often saw in it not so much the memorial of the death of the Lord as a kind of magic protecting them from earthly harm. As in the former case, Luther here identified a vulgar perversion of current practice with Catholicism itself, and made a clean sweep, rejecting the Mass as sacrifice and accepting only the Supper.

The same is to be said of his attitude towards those Sacraments which he thought he had to reject entirely, especially Extreme Unction. As we have seen, it was called in those days the Sacrament of the Rich, because only rich people could pay the high fees for it.

As the logical consequence of all this, Luther rejected along with the Sacraments those who dispensed them; he would have nothing of an official priesthood. It is true that his view of the priesthood of the laity was directly in line with his key-doctrine of salvation by faith alone. But it was not in fact because of such speculative theological considerations that he adopted this line and pursued it—he was not speculatively inclined, it was the rage of the reformer, wounded in his deepest religious sensibilities by the frightful degradation of the secular and regular clergy, that convinced him that the priesthood and the religious state were in themselves the origin and the bulwark of abuse, and that they must therefore be torn up by the roots.

But precisely because it was the abuses in the sacramental life that Luther had before his eyes, he never intended to attack the essence of the Sacraments themselves, the idea of the Sacraments in the Church. In other words, he did not mean to undermine the belief that heavenly gifts are exhibited to us and imparted to us in simple, earthly symbols. His confidence in the objective efficacy of the Sacraments is all the more striking in that the subjectivity of his belief concerning salvation must have exerted pressure on him in the opposite direction. And yet he clung to their objective efficacy. He made it clear that he believed that the miracle of grace by which saving faith is imparted is performed in the act of Baptism itself. For this reason he accepted infant Baptism from the Church's tradition, although infants cannot have trusting faith.

Similarly, in deliberate opposition to the "Sacramentarians", as he called Zwingli's followers, he associated the presence of the glorified Christ with the elements of the Eucharist; not, that is, directly with the subjective faith of the person receiving the Sacrament but with the objective faith of the Church, acknowledging the presence of Christ in these elements. When Luther, in his dispute with the Swiss Protestants, expressly

taught that even those who are personally unbelieving or unworthy receive the very Body of the Lord, he was testifying
in the clearest way to the ancient Catholic belief in the physical
as well as spiritual presence of our glorified Lord. It is something independent of the faith within the soul of the communi-
cant.

By retaining the Church's Sacrament of Penance—though
without the obligation to confess and without the performance
of satisfaction—by separating repentance from justification
and holding that justification was only completed in the act of
receiving the Sacrament, he was again giving decisive importance not to the trusting faith of the person alone but also
to the extra-personal, impersonal outward sign. Thus a round-
about way was opened for the reintroduction of a kind of
Sacrament of Penance, and as Harnack sarcastically says, "A
practice was created which was even worse, because laxer,
than the Roman confessional" (*History of Dogma*, 6th ed. p.
472).

In all these Sacraments it is a simple, visible sign that objectively guarantees the presence of the Holy One, the blessing of
the Redeemer. Thus through them the Church's *functionary*,
who performs this sign in the name of Christ and by the
Church's commission, necessarily in some sense re-enters the
domain of the supernatural, and acquires in some sense full
powers whose ultimate basis can only be an express decision
of our Lord's will and a special commission from Him. Thus
the old character of the Catholic priesthood still clings to
Luther's lay priesthood, in so far as an objectively efficacious
sign of grace necessarily implies a minister objectively and
effectively empowered to carry out this sign.

We cannot escape from the fact that wide tracts of Luther's
thought were simply Catholic. The people who eliminated

these Catholic elements from his message were the Lutheran theologians of the period of orthodoxy, especially in the late sixteenth and seventeenth centuries. There have always been on both sides theologians who, instead of protecting and promoting living religion, have endangered it. On both sides it has always been their habit to entangle living beliefs in bloodless abstractions, concepts and ideologies, and then to use the result as a ball to juggle with in polemic dispute. And when, having elaborated their systems of thought, they commit them to paper, it is usually with a bitter and choleric pen, and love is not in them. So it has always been. So it was then.

Luther himself, as we have seen, judged the doctrines, ordinances and usages of the Church according to their fitness for survival as he saw it: that is, according to whether they appeared to him to be loaded with gross abuses, or not. He suffered personally from the festering wounds in the Church and sought in his own fashion to heal them. It is true that he went about it, especially in the latter part of his life, with a self-assuredness and a cheerful readiness to assume responsibility which sometimes bordered on irresponsibility (Lortz I, 427). He was sometimes too ready simply to cut off the diseased limb instead of healing it. But his fundamental intention remained the healing and renewal of the ancient Church, not her dissolution and destruction. In the midst of his most violent attacks on Rome he said, "I may be mistaken; I am not a heretic" (Lortz I, 393). In the depths of his soul he was still, despite everything, bound to the Church, and that means to the Church as he then saw her, *ecclesia una, sancta, catholica et apostolica.*

We find a very different attitude in the orthodox theology which gradually developed and established itself. It took the

Lutheran doctrines out of their historical context, separated them from the ecclesiastical abuses with which they were bound up and presented them simply in themselves, as an abstract system of ideas, as the new Gospel in fundamental opposition to the old Gospel. Their expositions no longer envisaged the suffering Church, labouring under abuses, but simply the Church that had been. They were concerned to found and establish a completely new Church. Lutheran theology became radically anti-Catholic. It was therefore a special aim of their polemical writing to seize on all the Catholic elements which Luther had tolerated, and even expressly affirmed, and in the interests of the stylistic purity of their Lutheran doctrinal edifice ruthlessly to eliminate them. This de-Catholicising process was pushed so far that to-day, as we have seen, Lutheran theologians who wish to bring their people back to Luther's own vision of the Church are accused of Catholicising tendencies. Now indeed altar was set up against altar and Church against Church.

On the other hand, it is also true that modern Catholic theology in many important respects is determined by anti-Lutheran polemic. The Thomist and Scotist theologians of the pre-Lutheran age had been engaged in presenting and extending the ancient, classical doctrine received from the Fathers. The theology founded by Molina (d. 1600) of set purpose picked out precisely those truths which Luther had denied or distorted and formulated them in the sharpest possible opposition to Lutheran doctrinal opinion. Against Luther's doctrine of "grace alone" it strongly asserted the reality of human co-operation and described it as something active (*concursus simultaneus*). Against the Lutheran theory of the invisible Church it laid special stress on establishing the visibility of the Church and her functions, and especially on the primacy of the Pope. Against the Lutheran cry of "Honour to God alone!" (*Deus solus*), it laid strong emphasis on the rightness of honouring the saints, of the cult of Mary, and other things besides.

Thus to-day the tension, indeed the opposition, between Catholicism and Protestantism is felt and underlined more strongly by the theologians than it formerly was by Luther himself. We have to admit that on both sides theologians have had a great deal to do with deepening the differences between us, whether or not they may have been pushed into it by the current situation. And therefore rapprochement between Catholicism and Protestantism will only be possible *if it takes Luther as its starting point*. We must build from Luther outwards if we are to bridge the gulf between the Christian confessions. We can indeed boldly assert the paradox that it is only a determined return to Luther himself which will make it possible for our separated brethren to come home to their Mother the Church.

But—and this is the final consideration which seems to preclude the possibility of reunion—did not Luther himself, with unequalled savagery ("Grobianism" [1] was characteristic of the age, and in particular of Luther), attack the essential foundation of the Catholic Church, the "Rock" on which she is built? As early as the Leipzig Disputation in 1519 Luther had disputed the divine institution of the Papacy and its necessity for salvation, and from 1520 onwards he never tired of branding it as "the most poisonous abomination that the chief of Devils has sent upon the earth".

That is indeed so. Papacy had no bitterer, no more determined foe than the barefoot friar of Wittenberg. He converted opposition and even hatred towards the Papacy into an essential

---

[1] "Grobianism"—gross and brutal boorishness. (Trans.)

element of Protestantism. The Rock which supports and safe-guards the unity of the Church became in his teaching a rock on which that unity splits.

It is so to-day. There is no greater barrier to the union of German Christianity than the Roman Pope and his claim to have been called by God to be the Vicar of Christ and the Shepherd of all the faithful. All the theological difficulties that we have seen so far admit of at least a *possible* solution. But in this matter any such possibility seems excluded from the start. Why? Because in this matter not only men's minds but their very blood rise in revolt.

For centuries it was Germans who suffered most from the detestable strife which arose between the Papacy and the Emperors because of an unhappy confusion of religious and ecclesiastical issues with political and economic ones. The on-set of externalism and worldliness which accompanied the Avignon captivity was and is felt by those of the Lutheran faith in a far deeper sense than by us Catholics. *We* make a sharp distinction between the person and the office. *They* see the crying scandal of a prolonged outrage against the majesty of the Holy One, against the spirit of Christianity. Because their creed was born of the struggle against abuses identified with Catholicism, *protest* against the Catholic Church is an essential element of their whole religious attitude, the necessary found-ation of their independent existence. But even in those Protestant circles where religion no longer speaks with the accents of Luther, opposition to the Papacy is firmly rooted. There is no sense in hiding this. That passion for independent thought, for the autonomy of the intellect, which was en-grafted into the German soul by nineteenth century idealist philosophy, sees in every Papal command, every Roman decree, every book placed on the Index, a relapse into the

Middle Ages and a threat to the basic rights of the human spirit.

As we have already stated, there is no possibility of *any* Christian rapprochement with the prophets or believers of "free thought". They are too small and narrow for us, and, however much they rave about the freedom of the intellect, they are not free enough for us. They are too small and narrow for us because they shut themselves up from the start in the limited world of phenomena, the world of appearances. They put artificial blinkers on eyes open to unconditioned, eternal reality, because they will not see the real world, the world of God, which brings forth the visible world and maintains it in being. Plato would say that one of their eyes is missing, the eye that perceives what is above and beyond the senses, the Reality of realities, the Mind of all mind. We Christians cannot be content to share the vision of such moles. Even if the unfettered human intellect had attained to an understanding of all the forces and all the phenomena of this narrow little visible world and co-ordinated them in one system, we should feel in that system as in a cage. Again and again we should thrust our way through its bars to cry our *Sursum Corda*! For we Christians believe in a final, supreme meaning of all being and becoming. This Meaning is the living God. And we believe that the living God has opened Himself to us, in certain *homines religiosi*, the Patriarchs and Prophets, and at last in His Only-begotten Son; that He has opened to us the very depths of His being and of His inconceivable love. Standing within this love our souls can grow to their height and breadth. They grow free, incomparably freer than the purveyors of human freedom can ever become. For it is only in faith in the living God that we know that we are more excellent than the stream of cosmic forces and powers. We are above this stream, not below it. And it is only if we start from faith that we can read the riddle of existence and attain to a satisfactory understanding of the world and of ourselves. It is only because we are children of God that we are really free.

Union is only possible, then, where faith in the living God and His Incarnate Son still binds and strengthens consciences. It is only with *believing* Protestants that we can discuss this final decisive question: whether the Papacy was founded by the will of Christ, or whether it is Antichrist who has achieved an historical embodiment in it. For believing Christians this question can only be solved in the light of Revelation, only, that is, by listening in reverent fear to the Word of God, and to His Word alone, not to personal preferences and feelings. No anti-Roman sentiment should be allowed to decide the question for us or accompany our consideration of it. Ulrich von Hutten's diatribes against "foreign priests" are understandable against the background of the contemporary situation. All Germany was completely "anti-Roman" then, as the Papal Nuncio Aleander was himself compelled to report. The policy of the Curia in matters of finance and official appointments, and other things besides, had exasperated national instincts in the highest degree.

To-day there is no longer any just excuse for regarding the religious question from the point of view of national politics and giving it an answer in those terms. The Renaissance tendency in Rome broadly speaking came to an end with the frightful visitation of the *sacco di Roma*, when the Eternal City was laid waste in May 1527. The Council of Trent and the great reforming Popes, Pius V, Gregory XII and Sixtus V, finally eradicated the abuses within the Church. Not one of Luther's accusations could justly be made to-day. Even the political dealings of the Roman See with secular princes have become impossible. No sober theologian would to-day accept Gregory VII's *Dictatus papae*. The Gregorian system, resting on presuppositions completely alien to our own, can be finally relegated to the past. It was the result of the mediaeval view of the world. On a deeper level, it resulted from the fact that the unity of Western Christendom was created by Rome alone, that its maintenance through the centuries was due solely to the authority of the Roman Pope, that the Emperor himself owed his numinous aspect entirely to his coronation by the Pope, and that it was common Christian belief that all matters of political, economic and cultural policy were from the moral point of view (*ratione peccati*) subject to the authority of the Roman See. The rise of the principle of nationality and the national states cut away a considerable area from the Gregorian system, and it was finally superseded by the new idea of the world and humanity introduced by the Renaissance. In consequence it is not possible nowadays for a Lutheran to keep his eyes on the abuses of the late Middle Ages and speak of the papal Antichrist as a mainstay for his own religious position.

Since the Council of Trent the idea of the Papacy has been tremendously spiritualised. It has become strictly religious, strictly Christian, strictly ecclesiastical, and the glorious image of the Vicar of Christ shines out from all the illustrious figures that have adorned the Papal throne since the great reforming Popes. As things are now, the question of the divine rights of the Papacy can be decided for the faithful *only in the light of Revelation*. Since the believing Protestant, with the overwhelming majority of modern theologians, can not entertain doubts concerning the authenticity of Matt. xvi. 18–19, his conscience is clearly and seriously confronted by our Lord's words to Peter, ". . . I say to thee, that thou art the rock and upon this rock I will build my church, and the gates of Hell

E

shall not prevail against it, and I will give to thee the Keys of the Kingdom of Heaven." He must face up to these words.

From the purely Biblical point of view it is indeed possible for him to think here of Peter *only*, not his successors or in particular his successors in Rome. But he will not wish nor be able to deny that there is another possible interpretation. For Christ's words are valid for all time. They are words of eternity. If the first generation had need of a rock if it was not to be defeated by the gates of Hell, how much more would later centuries, threatened from all sides by schisms and heresies! Could Christ really have been considering only the few years in which Peter was to live? Would Christ not rather have been thinking of the Last Times which would be cut short by His coming and for which He wished to build an unconquerable Church? It is in any case *only in this sense* that Christianity afterwards understood Jesus' words concerning the rock and therefore called the See of Rome even from early Christian times the "See of Peter" (*cathedra Petri*). For it was convinced that Peter died as a martyr in Rome and was buried there, and that he lived on in his successors. It was in any case precisely the Church of Rome which from the time of Cyprian (d. 258), Irenaeus (d. 202) and even Ignatius of Antioch (d. circ. 110) was regarded as the chief Church of Christendom, as its true and unique centre of unity, creating and guaranteeing that unity.

As in the course of centuries the Church spread all over the world and the centrifugal forces, the forces of schism, grew stronger, so the inexhaustible vitality of the Church liberated centripetal forces too, and theologians understood more and more unambiguously and univocally the meaning of the Rock upon which Christ founded His Church. There is a great significance in the change which took place in the attitude of the greatest of the theologians of the end of the Middle Ages, the Cardinal Nicholas of Cusa. Like many of the theologians of the time, at the Councils of Constance and Basle he had, both in speech and in writing, supported Conciliarism, i.e., the superiority of a General Council to the Pope. But the lessons of Basle, the depressing realization that even the strongest religious desires do not prove themselves strong enough to create a unity of spirits, that there are situations so charged with explosive matter that even a General Council is no longer capable of reaching a united decision—all this drove him to the conclusion that amid the fluctuations of opinion there must be a last resort, a rock, to protect unity under *all* circumstances; a final, supreme religious authority, which *ex sese*, i.e., independently of the judgment of the bishops, can decide questions of faith and morals, and to which the whole Church is bound.

What Nicholas of Cusa discovered was to be learnt in the course of time by the whole of Christendom. We find ourselves confronted by the facts that alongside Luther appear Zwingli, Calvin and Thomas Münzer; that soon after Melanchthon's death the Lutheran Church was shaken by the crypto-Calvinists and Pietists; that in England, alongside the Anglican Church, Puritans, Presbyterians and Independents founded religious communions; and that to-day in America we can count more than three hundred sects tearing the Body of Christ to pieces. These facts practically force upon us the Catholic interpretation of Matt. xvi. 18, as finally developed at the Vatican Council in 1870.

It is the *inner necessity* of the Church, the constant threat and peril to her unity from human subjectivism, that necessitates this interpretation. For the sake of the unity of the Church the Rock of Peter's office must remain through the centuries, so that the Gates of Hell may not prevail. Seen from this viewpoint, the Roman Papacy and its claim to Apostolic authority cannot be an insuperable obstacle to the Christian confessions' coming together. For it is this Papacy alone which makes possible and realises what all of us Christians must strive for, spiritual unity amongst ourselves.

This brings us close to the answer to our third question: how is the unity of all Christians to be realised? It is the last question we have to discuss.

III

HOW IS REUNION TO BE ACHIEVED?

W E CONCLUDED our second lecture with the observation that the Catholic interpretation of Christ's commission to Peter—"Thou art the rock; upon this rock I will build my church"—arose out of the Church's need to maintain herself in existence against the centrifugal forces within her, or rather, that the interpretation was both prompted and confirmed by this need.

In fact, we can only speak in the full sense of unity in the Church if she stands upon *one* rock in submission to *one* shepherd. In the light of the development of the Western Church, this rock and this shepherd *can* only be the Bishop of Rome, whose See was hailed in the earliest Christian times as the *cathedra Petri*. Even distinguished Protestant historians like Salin and Kaspar do not attempt to deny that *belief* in the primacy, if not the *doctrine* of the primacy, goes back to the earliest Christian ages for which we have any evidence. The root of this belief is ultimately to be found in the early Christian view of the Church, in the conviction of the faithful that it was not they themselves, not their own Christian conscience nor their own interpretation of the Bible, but the authority of the Church alone that decided the question of salvation.

We have already pointed out that the first Christian communities were not founded by the written word but by the living teaching of the Apostles and their disciples, and that Christianity was already alive and flourishing before any Epistle or Gospel was written. From the beginning it was the *oral* teaching of the Apostles, not its crystallization in the Bible, which guaranteed the truth and clarity of the revelation.

From the literary point of view the Bible is a chance collection of missionary writings, inspired indeed by the Holy Ghost, but a chance collection nevertheless. It does not give a general view of revealed truths, a *Summa sacrae doctrinae* in the scholastic sense. Only in the Epistles to the Romans, the Ephesians and the Hebrews do we find a comprehensive development of ideas. But not even these Epistles give the whole of the Christian Gospel. Several of the apostolic letters have been lost, so that we have, for example, almost no information about the first eleven years of Paul's missionary activity.

The *whole* of revelation, the legacy of faith (*depositum fidei*) was entrusted from the beginning not to literary chance but to the personal responsibility of the Apostles and their successors. "O Timothy, keep that which is committed to thy trust," Paul exhorts his pupil (1 Tim. vi. 20). When the Gnostics appealed to mutilated or invented written texts, the decision against them did not come from Holy Writ but from the "rule of faith" (*regula fidei*), that is from the living, believing consciousness of the Church as preserved and transmitted by the Bishops. Luther's *exclusive* esteem and reverence for Holy Writ is in contradiction with the facts of history. From the beginning we find, welling up between Christ and the Scriptures, the living teaching of the Church, guarding and explaining the truth. Through every gap and rift in the Biblical message gleam the clear waters of the stream of tradition, coursing through the Christian communities, guided and preserved by the Bishops.

It is indeed *Christ* alone from Whom all the Church's teaching proceeds and to Whom it all points. Christianity is Christ. The teaching authority of the Church can do no more than draw on the riches of Christ. The Church has only to testify to the Lord's truth, not to create it. She is not herself the Light but is to give testimony of the Light. The Church's teaching activity is thus not creative. She generates no new truths of herself. She only takes the old truths, objectively given in Christ's revelation (explicitly or at the least in germ), and brings them into the subjective consciousness of the faithful.

The Church's formulation of these truths, her Dogma, is safeguarded by the Holy Ghost and therefore contains no error, but it is not inspired by Him. It is the expression, conditioned by historical factors and established by the Church's theologians—by human wisdom, therefore, though, as we have seen, safeguarded by God—of what revealed truth ultimately means. Thus the formulation is not precisely the same thing as the revealed truth itself. Revealed truth is unchangeable, given once for all; whereas, for the formulation, a development is possible and has indeed happened—a constant process of deepening and clarification in the course of the centuries. Yet, however much the Church's explicit teaching is and must be conditioned by the world of time, it is still infallible, contains no error, is guaranteed by Christ as His teaching, so that its connection with Him and His original message is closer and stronger than is either actual or possible within the Lutheran view.

We have arrived here at something essential which differentiates the Catholic from the Lutheran concept of the Church, and which provides the ultimate basis for the exclusiveness of

the Catholic Church, her claim to be the one means of salvation.
The believing Lutheran also recognises that he is bound to his
Church's confession of faith, to the ancient Christian creeds, to
the Confession of Augsburg, perhaps to Luther's *Schmalkala
Articles* and to the formula of 1580. But there is nothing absolute
about this tie: the believing Lutheran does not simply and
directly hear the word of Christ in the teaching of his Church.
It is truer to say that he does without the formularies of his
Church in his *own* experience of Christ, when he encounters
Him in his own conscience. And in so far as this experience of
Christ in each separate believer necessarily remains dominated
by subjective impressions, it is in the last analysis the *individual*
conscience that determines the form and colour of each man's
Christianity. His religious life does indeed gain something
from this subjectivity—an interior dynamism, pressure and
intensity; on the other hand, it lacks any ultimate assurance,
any unconditional guarantee that it is really Christ and His
Truth to Whom the believer has given himself.

It is a quite different matter with the certainty of the believing
Catholic. He is *unconditionally* bound to the teaching of the
Church, because he is penetrated with the certainty that in the
teaching of the Church he hears the word of Christ. He thus
identifies the Church's message with the Gospel of our Lord.
However humanly inadequate, however conditioned by the
times the formularies of the Church's teaching may be, they
are yet for the Catholic conscience, in their deepest content, in
their *substance*, brought out from the treasure of Christ.

In the strict sense this applies only to those truths which the
Church expressly proclaims as truths of revelation. In the
strict sense, then, it applies only to the realm of the Church's
dogmas. But in so far as these dogmas do not exist in intellectual
isolation but are connected both with each other and with truths

in the natural order, the light of faith shines also upon their whole logical and historical context, and guarantees its certainty with varying degrees of intensity and logical strength according to the degree with which it is bound up with the dogmas themselves.

Thus the Catholic finds himself in a universe of truths which is not the product of his own subjective experience but comes to him from outside, from the Church, who witnesses to these truths as truths of revelation. Within this universe he lives his religious life, the life of saving faith which acts by love. And he may either contemplate the whole of this universe with clear, conscious acceptance (*fide explicita*) or only assent to it in its main lines, its basic truths, and so cleave only implicitly (*fide implicita*) to the remaining parts of truth which are included amongst them.

We can easily understand that this universe of truths which is the fullness of Catholicism gives ground for misgivings to the Protestant committed to the bare evidence of Scripture. If Catholicism teaches that there is revelation apart from the Bible which we can gather from many sources, not always possible to check—from the decisions of Popes and Councils, of the Fathers and theologians, even from the unanimous beliefs and experiences of the body of the faithful, the *ecclesia orans*; if beyond Holy Scripture there is an ecclesiastical authority, constantly bound up with the present age, its views and its culture, which can decide on the revealed content of any tradition—does it not then become possible, even probable, that in the course of centuries of development the original gospel of the Lord will be contaminated from alien sources, and that Catholic dogma to-day differs in essentials from the message of Christ? Is it not the case, for example, that the devotion to God's Mother which is so lavishly cultivated in modern Catholicism and so abundantly supported from the theological point of view, was unknown in the first Christian centuries? And furthermore that many of the dogmatic statements of Mariology and their historical frame-work—including such details as the supposed names of Mary's parents, Joachim and Ann—originate from sources that were rejected as "apocryphal" by the early Church, by Jerome, Augustine, Innocent I and Pope Gelasius? Has not the so-called *Protoevangelium Jacobi*, which occupied the first place among the apocryphal writings of early Christianity, became almost a fifth Gospel for many devotees of Mary to-day? Does not the Church's teaching of the bodily assumption of Mary into Heaven, which will probably shortly become a formal dogma of the Church,[1] rest upon the so-called *Liber, qui appellatur transitus,* a book which was banished to the Apocrypha by Pope Gelasius in 495?

Seen from outside, these misgivings about the possibility that alien accretions may have contaminated the revealed content of the Church's tradition doubtless have weight. But not when seen from inside. Let us keep to our examples from Catholic Mariology. When the Church judges that a certain book is "apocryphal", this simply means that it cannot be counted as belonging to inspired Scripture, but does not mean that its evidence must be worthless from an historical point of view. Historical criticism must decide on its historical value.

It is certainly the unanimous opinion of such criticism that the Apocrypha we have mentioned are not to be be taken seriously as historical documents but are only pieces of anec-dotal story-telling whose sole purpose was edification. They were probably composed by pious preachers and catechists who wished to present certain ideas from Scripture and truths of the faith in a literary form so as to present them more forcefully

---

[1] The Dogma of the Assumption has been defined since this was written.

and impressively. In his essay "De la nature des évangiles apocryphes et de leur valeur hagiographique" (*Revue de l'histoire des religions*, 1932, p. 457), Père Saintyves makes an exhaustive demonstration of this. The events narrated in them cannot, therefore, be in any way regarded as sources of the Church's belief. Rather they *assume* that belief and in their primitive and clumsy fashion express it in images and fantasies.

Thus it was that when in the fourth and fifth centuries Mary began to be honoured not only, as hitherto, as the model of ascetics but as the virgin *Mother of God*, it was not these marvellous apocryphal tales but simply the decisions of the Councils of Nicaea and Ephesus which influenced the Mariology of the early Fathers. The Fathers of the Church clearly and completely rejected the Apocrypha; but just as clearly, and in the same writings, they drew from the decisions of the Councils the conclusion that Mary, in whose womb the Eternal Father's sole-begotten, consubstantial Son became Man, must be hailed as true Mother of God and as untouched, untouchable Virgin of Virgins; whose soul was sinless, whose body could no more be corrupted than that of her divine Son, and who as Mother of Christ embraced as a Mother all believers in Christ. It was these clear *Christological* truths and insights, arising out of the very heart of the Christian revelation, which fertilised the Mariology of the Fathers; certainly not unconfirmed legends about Mary. At the deepest level their Mariology was *applied Christology*. It is only these truths, inseparably bound up with belief in Christ Himself, which belong to the sphere of revealed faith—*not* those legends of Mary which circulate as "pious opinions" in popular devotion but are not confirmed in the dogmas of the Church.

And it is no different with the other truths of faith which have been formulated in the course of centuries by the Church, though not clearly expressed in the Bible. They are all contained at least in germ (*implicite*) in a revealed truth already clearly held and proclaimed by the teaching Church. They can all be shown to stand in an essential relationship to the Church's original, central dogma concerning Jesus the Christ. They have all, therefore, their assured place in the Christian message. They all had and have a salutary and creative effect upon the whole Christian body. They are all charged to-day with the devotion, the reverence and the atmosphere of living Christian faith. And we know that what lies behind all these dogmas is not the caprice of emotional piety nor mere historical chance but the clear teaching intention of the Church and behind her the message of Christ bearing testimony of Himself in her teaching.

We have come back to our starting point. We pointed out that the special character of the Catholic concept of the Church and the content of the Catholic faith lay in the identification of the Church's authority with the authority of Christ. The Church does not receive this authority indirectly, as though from the faith of the Christian communities honouring their Church as the teacher and witness of that faith. *Before* there were any communities with personal faith, and independently of them, when Christ founded His Church upon Peter, He constituted in Peter and with Peter the fullness of His own Messianic power. The Catholic sees in the office of teacher, priest and shepherd built upon Peter the continuation through the centuries of the Messianic authority of Christ Himself.

We must realise that, according to the testimony of the earliest sources, Christ did not attach this Messianic authority simply to the *personal* "pneuma" of His disciples, to their abundance of the spirit. They were not His Apostles simply by virtue of being His disciples. For this they needed a special *commission* from our Lord. "As the Father hath sent me, I also send you" (John xx. 21). This commission was given in the solemn act by which our Lord chose twelve from the multitude of His disciples to be His Apostles, exactly twelve, no more and no less, who were to transmit His Gospel to the twelve tribes of Israel. Thus our Lord organised the first Christian mission by the special call of the Twelve, the establishment of the college of Apostles. This college of Apostles is so much the one and only organ of the full powers of Christ that after Judas' suicide the election of Matthias had to take place to fill up the number of the Twelve. The fact that within this college, as we are shown in the Acts of the Apostles, Simon the son of John occupied a supereminent position, and that even in the Pauline communities he was referred to simply as "Rock", is not due to his personal qualities, to the strength of his faith, for instance, but again to a particular, explicit *call* by our Lord, which took place, as a consequence of the strength of his faith, in that solemn act at Caesarea Philippi (Matt. xvi. 18).

The very first Christian mission, the first preaching to the Jews, was not only a matter of the out-pouring of the Spirit but of institutional means established by our Lord Himself— the college of the Twelve and the office of Rock. And, in the same way, later on it was not simply to all Christians filled with the Spirit of the Lord, to all the men of the new faith and love, that the office of preaching the Gospel fell. On the contrary, unless an extraordinary charismatic gift gave evidence of their prophetic vocation, they must first receive *the laying on of hands* from the Apostles. It was only by this laying on of hands that they were numbered among the appointed witnesses of Christ (cf. Acts vi. 6; xiii. 3, etc.).

Thus from the beginning the spiritual basis of Christianity, its striving for the fullness of the spirit and interior perfection, was bound up with an *institutional* element, the connection of the plenitude of apostolic power with an impersonal super-personal act, the laying on of hands. This turns our attention away from the Self, from the personal qualities of the believer, and directs them to the authority of Christ, Who alone sends labourers into the vineyard and from Whom alone comes all redemption. What was later called the mission of the Church (*missio canonica*) was from the very beginning an essential element in the Christian message. "How shall they preach unless they be sent?" (Rom. x. 15). Only by the form of the laying on of hands did the believing Christian become a missionary, a witness of the word, a steward of the mysteries. He bears the full powers of Christ, but not so as to be in any sense autonomous and dependent on himself. He is in no sense the creative cause of our salvation, but only, as theology expresses it, the "instrumental cause" (*causa instrumentalis*) and visible tool chosen by the Lord of the Church, with which He, our divine human Redeemer, invisibly communicates to the faithful the salvation which proceeds from the Trinity. The laying on of hands simply but effectively expressed the fact that the missionary had his place within the whole mission of Christ and partook of His apostolic powers. By this means he entered the "apostolic succession", entered into physical and historical contact with the first disciples and with Christ Himself, from Whom every mission proceeds and Who alone is its meaning and its object.

It is thus with reverent pride that the Catholic looks back on the long line of his bishops, for he knows that there is not one among them who could not historically show that he had been received into that apostolic lineage and so had entered into direct contact with Christ Himself. It is this apostolic succession of his bishops which guarantees to him that the stream of Christian tradition which brought forth and sustains the Bible is no wild torrent to break its banks and mingle with alien currents but that it was received at the beginning and conducted on its way by a strictly constituted channel, the unbroken unity of this same apostolic succession, leading straight back to Christ and guaranteeing the purity of the tradition received from Him.

Seen thus from within, the Church is primarily an *institution for salvation*. She is not simply a community of salvation, a community, that is, which receives in faith the salvation of Christ and carries it out in herself. It is she who *gives* this salvation and makes the faithful members of Christ. Thus she stands not only in a passive but also in an active relationship to Christ and the salvation He gives—always of course only as instrumental cause, as the visible earthly tool with which the Lord of the Church, Who won her by His Blood, pours the treasures of grace and love proceeding from the Trinity into the body of the Church.

It is only because the Church is in this sense an institution for salvation that she can at the same time be a community of salvation. Her institutional, impersonal office constantly merges into the personal, the establishment of the Kingdom of God in the hearts of the faithful. The official side of the Church is never an end in itself, never self-idolatry, but always only a means and a *ministry*, a ministry to immortal souls. Simply because the Catholic sees in the Church's activity not the Church alone but ultimately Christ Himself at work, still teaching, still giving grace, still governing, his relationship to the official Church is a living religious thing, saturated with the same faith and the same love which he gives to Christ. What Eucken said of St. Augustine's concept of the Church is still true to-day of the life and experience of the Catholic:

"All authority and every development of ecclesiastical power is sustained and embraced in intense personal living. The person in his direct relationship with God remains the animating spirit of the whole. Out from this life with God and into the order of the Church flows a constant stream of power, warmth and fervour which keeps it from sinking into a soulless automatism of ceremonial practice and activism. It is not the brute force of authority working by the sheer weight of its mere existence; there is an inner necessity insisting upon authority and sustaining it. It is chiefly out of these deep wells of life that the Church draws the immense power over consciences which she exercises down to this present day" (*Die Lebensanschauungen der grossen Denker*, 9th ed., p. 241).

Catholicism means the closest possible fusion of the institutional and the personal, objective and subjective, office and spirit. And it is contrary to the essence of Catholicism when either of the two elements, whether the institutional or the personal, becomes exaggerated. In the balance of the two, in their organic relationship and interpenetration, lie the strength and life of the Catholic Church.

We must speak in more detail of this fundamental character of Catholicism if what follows is to be intelligible. The Catholic Church lives and breathes in the consciousness that by her apostolic succession founded upon Peter she stands in that stream of tradition which leads straight from Christ through the Apostles down to the present day. With this before her eyes she knows herself as divine tradition *incarnate*, as the visible embodiment of those powers of our Lord's Resurrection which are forever penetrating the world whether they were set down by the finger of God in Holy Writ or not. The Church has no need of witnesses. She witnesses to herself by the "divine tradition" in which she stands and by which she lives, indeed which she *is*.

It is indeed true that in the course of its long history many accretions have been added to the tradition which is safe-guarded by the apostolic succession, much that does not come directly from our Lord but was introduced by the Apostles or goes back only to the custom of the Church. The Church's theology, therefore, differentiates between the purely divine tradition (*traditio divina*), which actually came from Christ's own mouth, a purely apostolic tradition (*traditio mere apostolica*) and a purely ecclesiastical tradition (*traditio ecclesiastica*). But because both of these latter forms of tradition are of purely human origin she divides them sharply from that which has entered into her substance as the revelation of Christ, His own original words. The Church will not bind anyone to anything, and will not be bound to anything, except this divine tradition alone, this *traditio divina*.

Because of the way in which the message of Christ is thus united with her own tradition, the Catholic Church feels and knows herself as the Church of Christ in the emphatic, exclusive sense: as the visible revelation in space and time of the redemptive powers which proceed from Christ her Head, as the Body of Christ, as the *one means of salvation*. Because she is aware of this she is bound to condemn all other churches which have arisen or may arise—in so far as they are *churches*, i.e., sociological phenomena, and not merely a group of believers—as extra-Christian and indeed un-Christian and anti-Christian creations. To admit even the possibility that the final union of Christendom could take place other than in her and through her would be a denial and betrayal of her most precious knowledge that she is Christ's own Church. For her there is only one true union, reunion with herself.

Being aware of her mission she must, above all, anathematize
the opinion that the true Church of Christ existed only for the
first three centuries; that to-day she no longer exists, or at
least is no longer recognisable as the true Church of Christ.
According to this opinion, one must, as F. Heiler proposed,
strive for an ideal Church in which the Petrine-Roman type
and the Pauline-Protestant type are united and fulfilled in the
Johannine type. Or one must suppose that each of the Christian churches possesses a special charism, that each is building
up one particular side of true Christianity, that thus the whole
of Christian teaching will be achieved only by the union of all
the separate confessions. This was the so-called fragment
theory, which arose in the Anglican reunion movement as the
"branch theory"; the idea that it took the aggregate of the
separate churches to form a true Church of Christ, and that the
reunion movement was simply a matter of establishing a super-
structure of organisation over all the confessions, of founding
a sort of super-Church which would embrace all the separate
Christian communities with their particular creeds and rites.
According to Söderblom, for instance, the Catholic Church
consisted of three principal parts: the Orthodox-Catholic part,
the Roman-Catholic part and the Evangelical-Catholic part.

It is immediately obvious that because of her self-conscious-
ness the Catholic Church cannot recognize these branch theories
nor anything similar to them. And she is bound to reject
absolutely the opinion put forward by certain Protestant
theologians that being a Christian is simply a question of
accepting the "fundamental" articles of the faith, even simply
of accepting Christ, and not of receiving in faith all the truths
expressly or implicitly included in our Lord's teaching. And
it is the same once more with the suggestion put forward,
again by Archbishop Söderblom, at Stockholm in 1925, that

in the reunion movement stress should not be laid upon the *fides quae creditur*, the objective stability and authoritative assurance of the truths of revelation, but only on the *fides qua creditur*, subjective openness to the vital Christian values, a personal Christian experience.

All these possibilities had already been advanced in the second half of the last century by the Oxford Movement within the Anglican Church, in the hope of establishing upon this basis a reunion of Christian churches. They all started from the assumption that the Catholic Church was not the one true Church of Christ, and that thus a union of Christian Communions must be sought not in but *beyond* the Church. And it was therefore necessary even then—in 1864 and 1865— for the Catholic Church, because of what she knows herself to be, to reject completely any efforts at reunion along these lines and to forbid Catholics to take any public or private part in them. The prohibition was repeated even more clearly in 1919 in connection with the World Conference on "Practical Christianity" which was being planned to take place in Stockholm in 1925, and again in 1927 in connection with the World Conference on "Faith and Government" held that year at Lausanne.

To sum up all the past decisions on the subject, Pius XI issued on January 6th, 1926, an Encyclical *Mortalium animos*, which set forth a fundamental doctrinal treatment of the whole complex question from the Roman Catholic point of view. Though he paid tribute in it to the religious and moral ideals which inspired these efforts at inter-Christian reunion, he rejected with all the vigour of his apostolic authority the assumption that lay behind all these efforts, the equality in matters of dogma of all Christian confessions. Such equalising, he said, must necessarily lead to an indifferentism which would efface all truth and which would in the end reduce Christianity to a subjective emotional experience shorn of all the objectivity of Christian truth. The truth is that since Christ Himself is incarnate Truth and Reality, His Revelation too concerns objective *realities*, which remain eternally unchangeable quite independently of subjective experience. And because truth can only be one, it will not do to have Churches making mutually contradictory statements about the faith, although they call upon one and the same Christ. This means that the search for reunion is the search for the *truth*. This is why every attempt to achieve unity is such a serious matter, calling for a deep sense of responsibility towards God. The Pope solemnly declares: "Since the Mystical Body of Christ, the Church, is but one . . . it would be erroneous and foolish to say that His Mystical Body could consist of divided and scattered limbs. Whoever is not united with it, is united neither with the Church nor with Christ Who is her Head" (cf. M. Pribilla, S. J., *Um Kirchliche Einheit*, 1929, p. 224).

For the Catholic, in contrast to the Protestant conscience which is not in union with Rome, the *immediate* object of all effort at reunion can only be that each according to his powers should help to remove the obstacles which are keeping those who do not believe in her from the Mother Church.

For these obstacles are his responsibility as well. It is not as though it were only the non-Catholic Christian who was the guilty party while the Catholic could think of himself as completely innocent and magnanimously proffering forgiveness. We made ourselves clear in our first lecture: both are at fault, and this fault extends to Rome itself.

Pope Adrian VI made public confession of this through his legate Chieregato before the German Princes assembled at the Reichstag at Nuremberg on the 3rd January 1523: "We freely acknowledge that God has allowed this chastisement to come upon His Church because of the sins of men and especially because of the sins of priests and prelates. . . . We know well that for many years much that must be regarded with horror has come to pass in this Holy See: abuses in spiritual matters, transgressions against the Commandments; indeed, that every-thing has been gravely perverted." And therefore he authorises his legate to promise that "we will take all pains to reform, in the first place, the court of Rome, from which perhaps all these evils take their origin." When therefore the Holy See regards as one of its gravest and most urgent tasks the restora-tion of unity to Christendom—not only with the Orthodox Churches, which already have the essentials of dogma, cult and organization in common with it, but also with the Protestant communions—it is thereby fulfilling not only the duty of the Good Shepherd setting out in pursuit of the lost sheep but also the special duty of common penance and expiation.

Furthermore, it is not as if it were only the Protestants who are needy and the Catholics who are rich, overflowing with abundance and therefore able to wait contentedly until their starving brethren knock on their door. When these large portions of the Catholic Church were lost to her, she lost with them all those precious constructive powers, all those souls of deep religious aspiration who have since then worked so fruitfully and creatively within the separated communions, and who might have been called to cultivate the most perfect flowers of religious life upon Catholic soil. We lost much when we lost them. But the loss went deeper still.

Because large parts of western Christendom—in the tenth and eleventh centuries the Orthodox Greek-Russian Church with the Balkans, and in the sixteenth, considerable parts of

Germany, Sweden, Norway, part of Hungary, the Anglican
Church in England, Scotland and, dependent upon England,
colonial territories beyond Europe—because all these were
separated from Mother Church, her most dazzling, most
brilliant mark, her world-wide *Catholicity*, was in danger of
losing its former triumphant splendour. The world-wide
Church seemed to have shrunk to a community of the Celtic
and Latin peoples dwelling round the Mediterranean. And St.
Augustine's proud words seemed to have been belied: *In
omnibus linguis sum. Mea est Graeca, mea est Syra, mea est
Hebraea, mea est omnium gentium* (En. in ps. 147, 19). With
each schism the question arose like a threat: is our Church still
really Catholic to-day, really world-wide? Has she not
become a sect like the others? Because of the fearful seriousness
of the question we Catholics have every reason to do our share
in ensuring that the universality which, existing in germ, is
of the *essence* of our Church—her "*intensive* Catholicity"—
may be realised *extensively*; we must do our part to build her
up again across all the schisms and separations of the past,
that all men may see her for what she is, *Una Sancta*.

Moreover, this external, spatial catholicity of our Church is
closely bound up with her *internal* catholicity, the universality
of her spirit, the all-embracing character of her teaching.
Because she is, in her invisible, supernatural essence, identical
with the Body of Christ, all the religious and moral values of
Christianity have their source and their true home in her. They
are all destined, in their own time and place, to make their way
to the light by an organic process of growth, as the flowering
fruit-tree brings all the life flowing within it to its richest
development. But because the teaching Church, in combating
whatever heresies arise, has laid special emphasis on the truths
denied by those heresies, theological interest has tended to

concentrate upon these truths, to the hurt, or at least the weakening, of their organic unity with the other truths of the faith. All the more so since theologians have been somewhat chary of unearthing the germ of truth which, as St. Augustine repeatedly insisted, lies hidden in every heretical system.

Thus theology has not always been completely "catholic" in the original, classic sense of the word. It has tended instead to be anti-Arian, anti-Nestorian, anti-Monophysite, anti-Lutheran, anti-Modernist. It has been hemmed in by its opposition to the current heresy. The anti-Lutheran attitude taken up by theology in its battle with Lutheranism inevitably overflowed into the field of practical piety. So it came about that the believing Catholic, over against Lutheran individualism, set special store by the principle of the Church's *authority*, that here and there he let slip the sense of Christian freedom so precious to St. Paul, the sense of personal decision and responsibility. So it happened that he was in danger of regarding the whole of Christianity as a matter of mere blind obedience to the Church, and that consequently the Catholic attitude became one of passivity, even servility, of preferring to be led blindly rather than to see the road.

In the same way, opposition to Luther's cardinal doctrine of faith and grace alone not infrequently led to an over-emphasis, on the Catholic side, of sanctification by works and the externals of piety. The Catholic sometimes lost his way in a tangle of pious activity and neglected the most interior and essential matter, the simple "being in Christ" which abounds in trust, thanksgiving and joy. It seemed as though the justice of grace was to a great extent slipping back into a Judaic justice of works.

Only the fullness of *Una Sancta* will be able finally to overcome this anti-Lutheran attitude in Catholic devotion and to throw open again to souls the whole realm of revealed truth, including those truths and values at which the believing Catholic has for long looked askance because they were especially emphasized and exaggerated by Luther. Thus reunion with the separated Protestant Christians will always be an aim of first importance for Catholics too.

It was of course in the nature of the case that Luther's unrestrained attacks on the "papal Antichrist" and the subsequent bitterly anti-Catholic development of Protestantism, despite a few attempts at reconciliation, prevented any real will to understanding for many centuries. Rome held back. Reunion seemed completely hopeless. The only immediate course was to cast all care upon God. In his apostolic brief "Provida matris" in 1895 Pope Leo XIII dedicated the Novena of Prayer—the nine-days devotion before Pentecost—to prayer for the "Reunion of our separated brethren", and later on to the "Furthering of unity in Christendom". In 1908 the American Episcopalians started an octave of prayer with a similar intention, which Pius X approved in 1909. It is always kept from the 18th to the 25th of January, and Benedict XV extended it to the whole Church.

After the two World Wars, which showed with terrible clarity how the divisions between Christians prevented them from any effective effort to maintain world peace, the longing for an understanding between the Churches became more explicit and urgent. At Stockholm and Lausanne the Protestant communions sought to establish contact with the Greek Orthodox Church. And on all sides understanding of the Roman Catholic Church was growing too. When National Socialism began to display itself openly as anti-Christian and sought to realize this character in all its brutality, it was borne in upon every believing Christian that there was no longer any sense in poisoning the religious atmosphere by inter-confessional strife, and that the time had come to bear an *unanimous* witness to Christ. It was, then, the tragic events of recent history that prepared men's minds for religious discussion and understanding.

In what follows we will point out the basic principles which, from the Catholic point of view, must animate and guide every attempt at understanding and which alone can make our efforts at reunion fruitful.

We may lay down, as our first principle, that every serious intention of understanding presupposes *taking one's own Confession seriously*: an underlying readiness to give a strict account of one's own religious Confession in full realisation of one's responsibility before God. A man who has never taken his own church seriously is less likely to take any other church seriously. He has no ground for seeking another church if he has never taken the trouble to penetrate into the religious life and structure of his own Communion and to satisfy his religious needs there first. Religion is something so profound and so holy that of its very nature it obliges us in conscience to plumb the depths of our own Confession, to assay its whole content and know it in its entirety.

The history of Christianity has shown us that when the Enlightenment and German Idealism had weakened or loosened the basic content of belief, the consequence was indifferentism, and this indifferentism led in turn to a complete loss of Christianity. The reunion of Christendom is an eminently religious matter. Therefore it demands an attitude of mind that searches for light and truth for the sake of *religion*.

If a man attains to this clarity within his own church, if he can say Yes with complete conviction to his own church, he *may* not think of leaving it for another, he *may* not become a

Catholic. However objectively false, from the Catholic standpoint, his position may be, he is nevertheless subjectively bound to remain in it so long as his conscience compels him. For it is only the dictates of our own sovereign conscience that can transform an objective norm into a subjective duty. Every Christian must apply to himself the words of St. Paul: the just man liveth by faith (Rom. i. 17). That is to say, only the man who lives according to the convictions of his conscience is truly just. When a convinced Protestant Christian lives thus in union with Christ, he stands also in a relationship to the Mystical Body of the Saviour, of which indeed he had already become a member by the Sacrament of Baptism (cf. the Papal Encyclical, *Mystici Corporis*).

But where a man does not attain to this certainty of conscience, when an evangelical Christian finds that he has been mistaken, not indeed in Christ, but in his church, he finds himself, for the sake of truth, driven to leave his church in search of the true Church, and not to rest until he has found her. And he will find her, because the blessing of God, the strength and light of His Grace, will certainly fall upon such single-minded and fervent struggles for the truth.

But in either case, whether his relationship to his original Communion turns out to be positive or negative, a joyful affirmation or a critical rejection, he must take that Communion seriously, both as to its functions and as to its demands on him. This attitude is the only one which corresponds to the high ideal presented to us by the reunion of Christendom.

We thus come to the second principle which will ensure reunion or at least allow us to hope for it. It is this: our striving for unity cannot be a matter of politics or culture or aesthetics or romanticism. It must be a *religious* movement. Wherever our concern is with religion, it is first and foremost God Who is at work. Thus our movement must be primarily a movement of *prayer*. The Octave of Prayer from the 18th to the 25th of January, kept by all Christians, Catholics and Protestants alike, must not remain confined within the walls of our churches. It must not be a mere religious gesture. It is hallowed and sustained by our Lord's own intention, the final wish of His heart: *ut omnes unum sint*. It is the cry of all Christendom: *Exsurge Domine,* Arise, O Lord, enlighten our minds and set our hearts on fire, that all the hindrances of this world may fall away, that we may open our hearts to each other and go to meet each other. There is only one place where we can find each other: the Heart of Jesus. The way to unity is not from Peter to Christ but *from Christ to Peter*, not from the outer to the inner but from the inner to the outer.

The way is indeed harder for a Protestant than for a Catholic. As we have already said, a Catholic hears the words of our Lord directly in the words of the Church. He need only have ears to hear. And in the midst of his Church—though the outer walls show cracks and fissures, the traces of her long history—in the midst of her stand the Altars. They are enveloped with the Redemption of Christ, wreathed around with the seven holy Mysteries. In these Mysteries he meets Christ, person to Person. He feels in them the very heart-beats of our Lord. In Catholic churches there is not merely much talk of Christ; there is much prayer to Him. We live with Him in a holy communion of Flesh and Blood.

For a Protestant the word of the Church is not something final and supreme, the word of Christ Himself. To hear that he must go to the Bible. And since even the Bible only reveals the eternal word of the Lord in a form conditioned by the time, thus concealing it as much as revealing it, he must stretch his mind and heart to the utmost in an effort to experience Christ Himself, to penetrate through the letter of the Bible to spiritual understanding, to the reality, the very word of the Lord. Thus the Protestant is in the last analysis thrown back on himself.

But however much our two ways to Christ may differ, it is only by starting from Christ, only in the light of His divine presence, free from all worldly attachments, that we shall be able to see eternal truth naked and sheer, free from earthly taint, untouched by the longings and passions of our own hearts. It is only standing before Christ that we breathe pure air. The men and things that surround us then stand no longer in our sight but in His. We no longer see them with our eyes, but with His.

In the light of Christ the Catholic will no longer wish to regard Luther simply as an apostate who broke faith with the Church. He will recognize the many lights in his character: his unfathomable reverence for the mystery of God; his tremendous consciousness of his own sin; the holy defiance with which, as God's warrior, he faced abuse and simony; the heroism with which he risked his life for Christ's cause; and not least the natural simplicity and childlike quality of his whole manner of life and his personal piety. And, on the other hand, the Protestant's anti-Romanism can no more take root and flourish in the light of Christ than the Catholic's anti-Lutheranism. In the light of Christ the Protestant will realize that it was precisely the Papal power at its fullest development which gathered the world into the dominion of Christ; that it is this same power which prevents the graces of the Redemption which have come among men from being dissipated; that without Papal infallibility in matters of faith and morals the divine revelation would be for ever at the mercy of human error and extravagance; that the inner kernel of papal power, despite its external mediaeval splendour, is nothing but service of the Church, nothing but a perpetual washing of the feet of the disciples; and that upon the papal throne the succession of Peters has never died out, who to our Lord's question, "Peter, lovest thou Me more than these?" can give the simple answer, "Lord, Thou knowest that I love Thee!"

Wherever we look we see the same thing: unity with Christ is the only possible foundation for the unity of Christians. It is only out of this inner unity with Christ that external unity, unity with Peter, will grow—when God wills and as God wills.

We touch here on our third principle. This common love in Christ must bring all those who are concerned in *Una Sancta* to do what they can, with passionate determination, to soften the *antagonism* that exists between believers of the two Churches. There is no question here of concealing or minimizing the real differences in doctrine. On the contrary, for the sake of truth these differences must be laid bare, for this is the only way to reveal the true religious intentions which ultimately lie behind them on both sides. But these doctrinal differences can be presented quite objectively, and indeed in a truly eirenic form, directed towards mutual understanding. On the other hand, they can also be presented in an unreal and wounding form. Lutheran and Catholic controversial writing of the sixteenth and seventeenth centuries provides us with a shameful example.

Protestantism, in so far as it arose from a protest against Catholicism and therefore found itself compelled to build up its theology as a critical condemnation of Catholic doctrines in order to justify its own existence, is even more exposed to the danger of lapsing into this unreal style of polemic than is

Catholic theology. The latter does at least live upon the rich heritage of pre-Lutheran Patristic and Scholastic thought, and can build up the complete edifice of Catholic doctrine without any reference to Protestantism. Any expert in the matter will bear witness that Protestant scholarship, right down to the level of school text-books, is characterised by a much more savage tone than corresponding Catholic literature. On the other hand, there is a danger that the Catholic will be falsely influenced by the dogmatic intolerance of his Church, compelled, for the sake of truth, to condemn and reject all churches set up beside or against her, and will not bring to those of other faiths that openness of heart and true charity demanded by Christ.

There is thus on both sides a certain tendency towards loveless antagonism. There is an inclination to repeat old legends, long since exploded by serious research, like that of Luther's suicide, or of Pope Joan; or to argue from the crude expressions of naïve popular piety to the real doctrine of the Church; or to insist on dragging on with some general unfriendly feeling or prejudice against those of the opposite faith. Thus it comes about that Protestant and Catholic, though united by language and nationality and by thousands of cultural and economic ties, confront each other as strangers, not as brothers sharing their belief in Christ. And since they are usually most careful to avoid any talk of religious matters, contact at the deepest level is simply absent from their personal intercourse. This inevitably leads, on both sides, to an obscure feeling that the others are not being quite sincere and honest about it all. And this feeling may well poison mutual intercourse at its roots.

Wherever the ideal of *Una Sancta* is really alive, this miserable state of affairs, the most miserable part of the whole inheritance of schism, must be abolished completely. It cannot but be exasperating for a Protestant when someone glances at Luther's doctrine of salvation by faith alone and then speaks of "comfortable" Lutheran piety, contented with merely piously saying "Lord, Lord", as though Protestantism did not also stress the duty of penance and working at one's own sanctification. And it cannot but be exasperating for a Catholic to hear the holy Sacrifice of the Mass called a serving of idols, as though, for him, too, the Sacrifice of our Lord on the Cross were not the one, sole Sacrifice, which is made present for us at this moment by the Mass. It cannot but be exasperating for the Protestant when he sees Luther presented in the coarsest of pictures and regarded simply as a runaway monk; and it cannot but be exasperating for the Catholic when he finds Protestant text-books *still* devoting a paragraph to describing the Pope as the true Antichrist: etc., etc.

Trusting love, loving trust must be the animating principle of all our relations with each other, and especially of our religious literature and religious discussion. For where true love is, "love from a pure heart, and a good conscience, and an unfeigned faith" (1 Tim. 1. 5), there, and only there, is the Holy Ghost. We pray God that this spirit of openness of heart and trusting love may be active and fruitful also in those upon whom God's dispensation has laid the heavy duty of preserving the purity of the faith handed down by the Church. May they all keep for their guiding thread the prayer instituted by the Holy See for reunion with the Oriental Churches: "We pray thee, O Lord . . . keep us from any fault that might estrange us *yet further*."

To sum up: we must each take our own Confession seriously; we must each give ourselves unconditionally to Christ and His holy will; and, inspired by this love of Christ, we must each root out of ourselves all loveless prejudice against those of the other faith. These tasks in the religious and moral order are the necessary *a priori* preliminaries to any union between us, to any approach between Catholics and Protestants if it is to bear fruit.

How is this approach to be brought about in reality?

Because the Catholic Church knows that she is the one means of salvation, that she is sufficient to herself, that she witnesses to herself as Christ's teacher, that she alone among all churches has received the totality of the Christian revelation and alone hands it on, *no* approach to her can be made on the basis of bargaining in matters of faith (*in rebus fidei*) and effecting compromises, by which she renounces certain truths and is conceded others in exchange. Because the truth of Christ is one, the Church in her teaching must be intolerant to the utmost degree, to the very last article of faith. For truth is always intolerant. St. Augustine's words, " Hate error, love the erring!" is the Church's guiding principle in her care for souls. It is precisely out of her love for men that she is intolerant, because it is truth alone that can redeem us and make us free. There can therefore be no question of her ever giving up a dogma, i.e., a truth which she has declared to the faithful, with all the authority of her conscious teaching, to be revealed and presented to them for belief. In matters of faith she knows only of a clear Yes or No, never of an accommodating Yes *and* No!

There are, further, in the rich treasury of the faith which was left in her keeping, certain truths which, while they have all the maturity of dogmas, have not been elevated to actual formal dogmas. They stand, however, in such an intimate logical or historical relationship to dogmas already defined that they cannot be denied without hurt to those already laid down. These truths are so to speak making their way into the light. It is the *ecclesia orans*, the praying Church, which has for centuries carried these truths, guarded by the teaching Church, in her womb, bearing witness to them in her devotions and pious exercises long before the Church pronounced dogmatically on their revealed character.

Such truths are, for example, the bodily assumption of Mary into Heaven[1] and her mediatory power of intercession for all the faithful. The instinct of the faithful has always rejected the notion that Mary's immaculate body, from which came forth the glorified body of our Lord, could ever have turned to dust or become food for worms. And that Mary as Mother of Christ is also Mother of Christians, embracing in her loving intercession the whole of the Mystical Body of the Lord, has always, both in the East and in the West, been the centre and key to all devotion to her. It would not be difficult to demonstrate this same belief in Mary's all-embracing intercession from Luther's sermons on her.

Thus these truths lie in the subconscious mind of the Church and at the same time ripen towards the full maturity of her dogmatic teaching. The truths of revelation are not something dead which are handed on by some external mechanical process. They are vital principles, with their roots in the spiritual world and in the needs of humanity, and so develop till they come to their full flowering.

But, on the other hand, it is easily understandable that a dogmatic promulgation of such truths would put a heavy burden on Protestant consciences otherwise disposed towards reunion. For the Bible is silent concerning them. They are only implicitly contained in the scriptural passages about Mary, and were elaborated only by the Church's tradition. But the Protestant conscience stops short at the words of the Bible

[1] The Dogma of the Assumption has been defined since this was written.

G

and feels oppressed by each new dogma of the Church that goes beyond the Bible. Should the Church, in loving compassion for the hesitancy of our Protestant Brethren, set aside the solemn definition of these truths, although it has long been expected by the majority of the faithful? Should she thus follow, in the matter of devotion to Mary, St. Paul's principle that the "weak in faith" should be given, not "strong meat", but "milk"? Or does the majesty of God's word demand that silence be broken, that, as soon as a truth has come to maturity in the consciousness of the Church and the faithful, its whole fulness should be made known, "in season, out of season" (2 Tim. iv. 2)? This is something that the teaching Church alone can decide. We Catholics have confidence in the Holy Ghost, Who lives in the whole Church, Who leads her into all truth and guards her from all error. We have confidence that at the right time He will communicate to our spiritual leaders what they are to say and what they are not to say.

This raises the all-important question: does what we have been saying mean that in the event of a reunion the Catholic is to remain in undisputed possession of *his* beliefs, whereas the Protestant is to abandon and even deny those truths which are characteristic of his religion and especially dear to him? This is a question that touches us in our inmost conscience. The question of reunion stands or falls by our answer to it.

We have already made it clear that a Protestant who is thoroughly convinced of the rightness of his religion may not become a Catholic. We are about to enter upon a most delicate matter, and I must beg forgiveness in advance if I am treading too boldly. But what, seriously, is the state of the Protestant's belief, of the extent, the vitality and the firmness of his faith? More than four hundred years have passed since Luther's day. Because of Luther's own basic subjectivism his gospel was bound to develop in very different and even contradictory ways under different subjective influences. Right at the beginning the Calvinist and Zwinglian types of Protestant were so different from the Lutheran type that the Lutherans in Saxony considered it their duty to sentence Councillor Nicholas Krell, the leader of the crypto-Calvinist movement, to ten years' imprisonment.

But differences soon began to arise within Lutheranism itself. Pietism and similar revivalist movements gave rise in Germany to the Herrnhut Brotherhood. The Anglican Church produced Methodism, the Salvation Army and others besides. The course of Protestant development led on the one side to Schleiermacher's theology of feeling and on the other to the Higher Criticism and rationalistic "Enlightenment". From the Enlightenment the road lay open to German Idealism, and Nietzsche even called Luther the "Grandfather of German Idealism". We do not need to point out in detail how nefarious and even catastrophic have been the effects past and present of German Idealism on the old faith and its theology. Nowadays there is even talk of an "unending Reformation" of a "Church in a state of Becoming", knowing no final pronouncements on anything, using forms of worship that are neither one thing nor the other, and aiming at being "A Church for non-churchmen" (cf. F. Parpert *Die endlose Reformation*, 1939).

The subjective principle in Protestantism became more and more obviously a principle of self-dissolution. It was thus inevitable that those who still set store by the objective stability of Christianity should find their eyes automatically turning towards the Church in which this objectivity is securely founded and has attained to a visible form, the Church of Rome, whose apostolic succession constantly guarantees her as the direct heir of primitive Christianity. Even if such a recognition meant that treasured memories must be sacrificed, even if conscience demanded that the first-born, Isaac, the only son, must be laid upon God's Altar, still no price is too high for the truth. But *it is not even the case* that reunion demands such a victim.

From the Catholic point of view it is *impossible* that any true religious experience should ever have to be excluded from the Church's embrace. The Church can and certainly will reject any formula that contradicts any of her dogmas or the spirit of them. But it can never be that along with such formulas she will judge and condemn the religious experiences that lie behind them, so long as these experiences are genuine, i.e., so long as they have their origin in Christ's message and breathe His Spirit. Whatever proceeds from Christ and leads back to Christ has its true home in the Catholic Church. There is no true religious value which does not, or could not, find its roots in her. She is wide enough and rich enough to fulfil and satisfy in herself every true and genuine human aspiration growing out of the depths of Christian consciousness.

It may indeed happen that at times when heresy arises the teaching Church, so as to present a firm front against error, is compelled to eliminate or set aside not only the heresy itself but any formulas, experiences and aspirations that have attached themselves to it, even those with a genuine and approved content of truth. When Arianism arose, for example, the old trinitarian doxology, so full of meaning—"Glory be to the Father, through the Son, in the Holy Ghost!"—was altered to "Glory be to the Father and to the Son and to the Holy Ghost!" because there was a risk that the expression "through the Son" might be taken to imply an Arian subordination of the Son to the Father, instead of attributing to Him equality in being with the Father.

Similar displacements of the balance of dogmatic truths took place in the struggle against Luther and later on in the struggle against Modernism. Faced with Luther's doctrine of faith and "grace alone", Catholic theologians no longer, as hitherto, laid their greatest emphasis on the spiritual constitution of the Church, the *communio sanctorum*, but on her external aspect as an institution for salvation and on her hierarchical constitution. And in the arguments with Modernism, which interpreted faith simply as a felt experience, the teaching Church underlined the intellectual aspect of faith, faith as an act of the understanding, and not so much, as before, faith as an act of the will and a work of grace.

It is only when the danger to the Church's doctrine from a particular heresy is past that the original balance between the dogmas, their own internal harmony, automatically re-asserts itself. Since no heresy is *simply* error, but is always characterised by the over-emphasis and exaggeration of some particular truth, later, when the danger from the heresy is overcome, this core of truth will come to light again. *But it is precisely this real core of truth which enkindled true religious experience and true religious aspiration.* As long as the Church has to oppose heresy such aspiration must shine only with a quiet and modest light, as it were behind a bushel. For so long as it is bound up with open heresy, its public vindication would lead to misunderstanding, and the Church cannot therefore permit it. But the time will come when it is taken out from behind the bushel and set on the candlestick. For it is simply impossible that in the Church, which is "the pillar and ground of truth" (1 Tim. iii. 15) any religious truth, any religious value, any religious aspiration could be permanently oppressed or restricted.

A Protestant who is disposed towards reunion need not fear,

therefore, that joining the Catholic Church will cause damage to his soul, in spite or rather *because* of her zeal in defence of the treasure of the faith and her repudiation of any compromise in matters of belief.

But all this will make her all the more generously and magnanimously ready to make concessions in matters of discipline (*in rebus disciplinae*), i.e., in the application of the faith to current life, in the whole field of Church discipline and ecclesiastical practice. Because there is no question here of revealed truths, of truths of God, which are infallible and unalterable, but of purely ecclesiastical ordinances and laws—decisions arising from the Church's needs at a particular moment, in fact, and therefore alterable—it is always open to the Church in her pastoral office to withdraw such regulations according to circumstances of time and place, to alter them or to introduce new ones. The Catholic knows that where it is a matter of the interests of the Christian faith the Church, in her pastoral office too, is protected by the Holy Ghost against making wrong decisions. But he knows too that regulations of this kind, unlike the eternal standards of the faith itself, are closely related to their own particular age. Thus they have only a relative value, and when the flowing stream of time has brought new men, new relationships and new situations to the surface, they may have to undergo changes.

If God should grant that whole communities, whole territories, even whole churches should enter into internal and external union with the Roman Church, so that the question was not one of individual conversions but of *corporate* reunion, a situation would arise in which the authorities of the Church would have to decide on considerable alterations in disciplinary regulations, at least for the newly-incorporated communities. The clergy involved would in all probability remain true to their pastoral calling. On the other hand, many of them would be married and not disposed to leave their wives and children. Rome might, then, for these parts of the Church, withdraw or at least restrict her law of celibacy, which forbids married life to her priests, just as she withdrew the same law for the Uniate Orthodox-Catholic communities of the Ukraine. The need for unity in disciplinary matters would make this impossible in individual cases, but for united bodies it would be admissible.

It is possible, however, to think of other ways in which the Church could meet outsiders half-way. For example: the diaconate, which Wichern introduced into the Lutheran Church, and which has always had the status of a sacrament in the Catholic Church, might be built up again, as in early Christian times, into an independent office in the Church. Deacons could be entrusted with the pastoral duties of preaching, the administration of Baptism and Communion, religious instruction and the dispensing of charity. Convert Protestant clergy would then, seen from without, continue to have the same duties which they carried out in the Protestant Church. Seen from within, they would have a share in the sacramental order of the Church. As distinct from the priesthood itself, which would have charge of the more intimate care of souls, the celebration of Mass, and the Confessional, the diaconate could be exempted from the law of celibacy. But however it might be done, it would certainly be made possible for convert Protestant clergy to take part in the care of souls without their having to shoulder burdens too heavy for them.

The reunion of whole communions would mean too that values in the care of souls which are specially cultivated in the Protestant churches, and which do not exhale an anti-Catholic or un-Catholic atmosphere, would be taken into the Catholic

Church. In living intercourse with similar Catholic customs they would infuse new life into the pastoral activity and the piety of the Church and make a real contribution to it. Thus as the French Dominican J. Kopf said in his review of the oecumenical movement (*Dokumente*, 1947, Vol. 6, p. 316), "the reunion of the Church will not only repair the wrong of schism" but will mean "the building up of a new, more embracing, richer unity than was there in the first place, a unity which will really have taken into itself new human values. It will be an *advance* upon the situation that preceded the schism. This universal Church of all Christians will be something new in the sense that the oak is something new in relation to the acorn—in full and perpetual unity, that is, with the Church of the Apostles. . . . If reunion comes it will come at a *maximum* level, not at a minimum, in abundance, not in poverty."

No one will deny that Protestant theology, wherever it has preserved *belief*, has not only rendered great services in the fields of religious history, religious psychology, the history of dogma and Bible studies but that its deep penetration of the actual, concrete life and work of our Lord and its critical reconstructions of the historical background to them have helped to bring the figure of Christ very much closer to present-day people. And by its impressive insistence on giving the Church and theology their place *under the Cross* it has done its part to deepen the Christian awareness that the message of Jesus is eschatological in its orientation, that it looks towards the Last Things and the second coming of Christ; and thus to guard against the delusion that Christ's Church is already, in this world, a Church of glory instead of a Church of humiliation, carrying the Cross after her Lord and Saviour.

Along with its theology, a reunited Protestant communion

would bring into union with Catholic values its own other great value, its Biblical interests and inclinations. The spread of the Bible through the whole world is primarily due to Protestant efforts, and it cannot be denied that, in spite of the happy advance of Biblical activity in the Catholic Church, and bearing in mind that knowing the Bible does not necessarily mean knowing the faith, familiarity with the Bible is more deeply rooted, richer and more vital in Protestant communities than with us. Therefore our drawing nearer to each other will give Catholics a fresh impulse toward seeking for Christian truth where it is to be found in its primitive apostolic form.

From the Bible and the piety it inspired there has grown the evangelical form of Church music, the Chorale. Its expressive beauty and power and its devotional content will continue to sing themselves into the hearts of Catholics who are already well acquainted with much evangelical Church music. If reunion comes, this music, with its deeply religious character, could play an important part in showing both Catholics and Protestants how closely, at the deepest level, their faith and love touch each other.

Closely bound up with theology, the Bible, and the Church's music is *divine service*. It is here that the Catholic Church is revealed in her greatest beauty and can, on her side, most richly endow her returning children. For the Mass is that supreme mystery which brings the one, unrepeatable sacrifice of the Redeemer in ritual form into our moment, into our here-and-now. Her seven Sacraments too have no other meaning, no other aim, than by simple, visible signs to make our Saviour present to us in His saving, pardoning, redeeming activity. It is thus in the mysteries of the Catholic Church that Christ our Lord steps out of the distant past straight into our own present. Through them, Christianity changes from a movement of yesterday into an event and experience of to-day. Catholic Churches are places of prayer and personal union with the Redeemer.

It will probably be a difficulty at first for a Protestant that the Church celebrates her services in a foreign language, Latin. But let him remember that this is the language of the Mother Church from which all the West received Christianity; and that it is a religious language, hallowed by use through so many Christian centuries, and lifted above the passage of time, immune from passing fashion and worldly corruption and misuse by the spirit of modernity. In addition to which, the Catholic Church has always been broad-minded enough to permit those reunited communities who wished to do so to keep their traditional liturgical language.

Apart from the liturgical language, our brothers and sisters returning to the Mother Church will no doubt be taken aback by the many *ceremonies*, the rich external pomp and splendour with which the Catholic Church has surrounded the Holy of Holies. To an outsider much of it may seem unintelligible and exaggerated, especially those ceremonies originating from the pomp-loving Greek-Oriental rite. In reality what shines out from this is the Church's love for her holy mysteries and her zealous endeavour visibly to present them and their deep significance to the faithful in their *otherness*, their heavenly character. Every vestment the priest wears, every gesture he makes, is a symbol and a reminder to the initiate that here in the Holy Place his concern is not with the earthly and human but with the holy and divine.

The Mass stands in the centre of Catholic worship. Around it cluster as it were a flowering garland of devotional practices: devotions to the Sacred Heart of Jesus, the Way of the Cross, devotions to Our Lady, the Rosary. And around these are grouped processions, pilgrimages and so on. It is easy to understand that long public prayers, poured out through awkwardly mumbling lips from simple, unsophisticated hearts, produce a repellent rather than edifying effect on the outsider and give the impression that they are lacking in serious piety. But one who knows the soul of the Catholic people will judge differently. For he knows to how great an extent this apparently quite external prayer is borne along by a profound, though gentle, undercurrent which in its very depths is directed towards God and pours itself unstintingly into God. Its inmost heart is thus numinous, sanctified all through by the Holy Ghost. It is like the prayer of the mother of Samuel, whom the High Priest Heli suspected of being drunk because only meaningless sounds fell from her trembling lips, whereas in reality her soul was torn by deep anguish and was crying to God for help.

Furthermore it must always be remembered that all these devotions, litanies of the saints, indulgenced prayers, pilgrimages and so on are in no sense *commanded* by the Church but only *commended*. The Church simply declares that, rightly understood, they are useful and salutary. It is entirely at the discretion of the believer to decide whether he will practise devotions of this kind or not. The devotional life of the Church is penetrated with a spirit of limitless individual freedom. This spirit of freedom will always manifest itself in new forms, in countless new devotional practices, innumerable as the leaves on a tree.

We can say with certainty that if ever a lasting union between the Catholic church and the Protestant communions were to take place, there would be a giving and receiving of gifts on both sides. It would be quite impossible that one single item of truly Christian value could be lost.

It is, of course, true that as things are at present any mutual approach will be only at first from person to person, not from Church to Church. It will at first be individual conversions which will build up the movement of reunion. But even in these conversions we begin to see the tremendous fruitfulness of that final synthesis, the harmonious union of Protestant simplicity with Catholic richness, Protestant gravity with Catholic joyousness, Protestant recourse to the Bible with Catholic faith in the Church.

Thus it is from the religion of converts in particular that a ray will shine out, lighting up the way which the churches themselves will later follow, if God grants it. A friend has made available to me a declaration which the well-known convert and writer Fräulein Gertrud von Zezschwitz wrote with her own hand upon her death-bed. She died in January 1946. She wrote: "The Catholic Church is worth every sacrifice. In twenty-seven years she has made up to me for each and every one of them and to my last breath she will continue to strengthen and console me. Only one who belongs to the Catholic Church and has grown right into her can value her aright. . . . With all her humanity she does not belie her divine origin, and she has thus been able to overcome her periods of decline and to go forward from them renewed." To this testimony Fräulein Zezschwitz joined the Lutheran prayer of blessing: "So do I remain ever with Thee, my God. For thou holdest me by Thy right hand. Thou leadest me with Thy counsel . . . If I have but Thee, I ask for nothing in Heaven or upon earth." Lutheran Biblical piety, and faith in the Catholic Church, are most intimately united in this dying testament. Indeed, they are *one*. Here we see a new way in which unity, *Una Sancta*, utters itself.

Well do we know that at first it will only be individuals who seek and find this road to the Mother Church. There can be no expectation of corporate reunion in the near future. For corporations, communities, churches, as collective entities, obey not only religious but also sociological laws. They are tied to common doctrines, a common theology, a common worship, common ecclesiastical institutions. Their members are woven into the same social and cultural complex of relationships and embedded in the same customs. Because of their common experiences and their common history they have developed a strong inner core of ideas. Thus they have a soul of their own as communities, a spirit of their own which consciously stands out against the ruling spirit of other communities, and which grows stronger in proportion as consciousness of its different and contrasting nature grows clearer.

Thus the Christian churches, simply because they are sociological phenomena, corporate entities, face each other as irreconcilable strangers. From the purely human point of view we can say that it will surely never happen, that the churches by their own free decision and in accordance with a radical change in their own inner attitude, will break their shells and set their followers free. This would only happen involuntarily, through some superior force, as, for example, if a religious communion were compelled to it by a mass exodus of its members or because external events brought down its house about its ears. At least, this is true from the purely human point of view. But *the thoughts of men are not the thoughts of God.* Who has known the mind of the Lord? Therefore, we may and must hope against all hope; He will hear us, if only we will entreat Him. He will open roads to us whose entrance and exit are still hidden from us in darkness. We will echo the confidence of Bishop Buchberger of Regensburg: "One day we shall be heard, one day there will again be one flock and one shepherd."

Perhaps God's wisdom, omnipotence and goodness demand that first we Christians must *all* descend into the Catacombs, that days of terror and of night must come upon us before we can see each other's hearts and call each other brother and sister. Or perhaps God will send us a Saint, a glowing, shining soul like St. Francis of old, to open our clenched hands and clasp them in each other's. The legend of the "Pastor Angelicus", the angelic Shepherd of the Last Days, has run through Catholic Christendom for centuries. We do not know what is in the divine plan of salvation.

But we do know that we ourselves, though we cannot create any final unity in Christendom, must do everything possible to prepare the way for *dynamic* unity, a unity of hearts and minds. If there cannot immediately be unity of faith, let there at least be unity of love. And this love must and will drive us to work in common in public life and to make common cause in our social, cultural, economic and political duties and interests. Nothing but this unity in love can provide the prerequisite foundation for our future unity in faith. It is then not only a moral but also a religious duty. As faith leads to love, so does love to faith.

In the oldest Christian liturgical document that has come down to us, the Didache, the community prays, thinking of the heavenly Bread prepared upon the Altar: "As this bread was scattered upon the mountains and has now been gathered together, so may Thy Church be gathered together from the ends of the earth into Thy Kingdom. For Thine is the glory and the power through Jesus Christ for ever more."

This prayer of the first Christians is our prayer to-day. So be it. God grant it. For all Christians *one* God, *one* Christ, *one* faith, *one* baptism, *one* Church,

UNA SANCTA.

Publisher: Sheed + Ward

Title: One and Holy

Author: Karl Adam

Cam No.: 1

Date: 14-3-55

(Student's Name)